Britons Into Battle

NOBODY really knows how armour came into being or who were the first fighting men to wear it. It was probably discovered by accident by primitive people whose first piece of "armour" was quite possibly a shield they used for protection against the spears and arrows of a rival tribe.

These early shields would almost certainly have been made of withies woven in basket-work fashion. Later they would have been covered with animal skins. It is doubtful, however, if these early ancestors of ours ever used any kind of body armour. Armour as we understand it today only arrived with the Bronze Age when men learned how to work in metals, and began to make pieces of protective armour to save themselves from serious wounds in battle. Helmets of bronze were worn by Sumerians 4,500 years ago. A collection of model soldiers found in a tomb dating back over 4,000 years shows that the ancient Egyptians used hide covered shields, and went into battle with bronze tipped spears. Centuries later the formidable professional armies of the Assyrians employed infantry wearing body armour, bronze helmets and carrying shields. Metal helmets, breast plates, and greaves, or sheaths of metal to protect the legs, were worn by ancient Greeks.

When men began to work in iron it did not immediately replace bronze but was used for sword blades, axes and spear heads. Body armour in early times usually consisted of helmets, breast plates and back plates each cast or beaten from a single piece of bronze, but sometimes was made of smaller pieces laced together. Mail, that is iron rings linked together to form a flexible garment was known in Roman times and continued in use for centuries. The legionary of Roman times seldom wore mail however. He was clad in a cuirass and shoulder guards made from metal strips. This was the "LORICA SEGMENTATA", and was a fairly flexible defence. An excellent helmet made of bronze with peak, neck guard and ear flaps completed the armour none of which was worn on the legs, for the legionary was a great route marcher!

The first iron helmets were made from four or more pieces rivetted together. This type of headgear was worn by Norman soldiers who came over with William the Conqueror in 1066. Norman horsemen wore short sleeved mail shirts of knee length with a hood of mail under the helmet. The warrior's defence was completed by a long wooden shield. Mail gave quite a reasonable protection, but if a man received a powerful blow from a sword or mace the mesh could be driven into the flesh resulting in a more serious wound than might have occurred had no armour been worn. Because of this a padded or quilted garment was worn beneath the mail. Mail was worn by knights

At the battle of Hastings in 1066 it was Norman versus Saxon—and both sides relied on mail for their protection.

The picture above shows Richard I with his troops. By this period helmets had begun to develop from the "Norman" type to the pot or barrel shape.
Left: a knight of about 1300—10 wearing armour that has had plates added. The helm is now a better pointed shape.

and foot soldiers during the 12th and 13th Centuries. During the Crusades Richard the Lion Heart would have worn it with the addition of mail stockings. About this time the helmet of the mounted man was deepened to protect the face and later the back of the neck.

In the 13th Century plate armour began to be worn. Wealthier warriors wore beneath their mail the "coat of plates", a sleeveless jacket of cloth with iron plates rivetted inside it. This was obviously a defence against the lance wielded by an opposing knight. Vulnerable knees were next protected from the foot soldier by "poleyns" of iron and soon after the beginning of the 14th Century, plates of iron were being strapped over the mail on arms, legs and feet.

Between 1300 and 1400 the mounted knight changed from armour of mail to armour of plate. Like all great conflicts since then the Hundred Years War between England and France gave rise to great changes and developments in body armour and weapons.

Armourers became so skilful that

"plate armour" could be fashioned to fit the wealthy patron from head to foot in steel that fitted almost like a glove but was so jointed as to allow free movement to every part of the body. A great deal is known about this type of armour, not only from old manuscripts but also from the many almost perfectly preserved examples, some even from the early 15th Century, which still exist. A later but most interesting suit of armour to have come down to us is one made for Henry VIII which can be seen in the Tower of London.

This particular armour was "tailor" made for King Henry, and shows us that he had a somewhat portly figure! He is seen sitting astride his charger which has its own body armour. Dressing a man in full plate armour took some time, and the various pieces needed to be put on in a certain order. Each piece had a name, such as greaves, or shin pieces; poleyns, or knee pieces; cuisses, or upper leg pieces; tassets, or thigh pieces; cuirass—breast and back plates; vambraces, or covers for the forearm; couter, at each elbow; and a gorget to protect the neck. Even the hands were protected by jointed steel gauntlets, and, of course, the head by a helmet usually with a visor that could be raised or lowered.

Armour was expensive to make and only wealthy people could afford to have an elaborate suit made. It is also important to remember that as designs improved two types of armour were developed —one which was used for battle, and another heavier type used in the sports of the tiltyard. Because of its discomfort and weight it was never possible to wear complete armour for long, particularly when vigorous fighting had to be done. There are records which show that men had great difficulty in remounting a horse should they be knocked off it in battle, and often found it no easy task just to get back on their feet!

Young knights competing in the "lists", when they would ride full pelt at each other with lances, frequently wore complete armour, and sometimes additional pieces were added for protection. The metal used for this "sporting" armour was often thicker than that used on the battle field, and it gave the wearer an opportunity for "showing off" by having his suit engraved and even covered with gold leaf! Armour with traces of gold leaf still exists.

The weight of armour varies considerably depending upon a number of things such as the thickness of the metal used, the skill of the armourer etc. An engraved suit made for Henry VIII and which was

By the time of Edward, the Black Prince, the use of mail in armour had been greatly reduced and was mostly plate (right). Below: during the Wars of the Roses complete plate armour was worn by knights. Foot soldiers were better armed— on the left of the picture an early hand gun is being used.

Henry the VIII, suitably protected by armour, is seen above taking part in a jousting contest, watched by his wife Catherine of Aragon. On the left is armour worn by Henry as a young man in 1514 and on the right is illustrated armour worn by him in 1535—by which time he had increased a little in size!

intended as a fighting outfit weighed a total of 28 kilograms (63 lbs 11 ozs) including the helmet, while a tilting suit made for the Earl of Worcester weighed an incredible 46 kilograms (103 lbs). Helmets weighed between 3 and 4 kilograms (8 and 10 lbs) and must have given their wearers neck-ache after a few hours. A full suit of armour was far too heavy for a man to fight on foot while wearing it, so he had to be mounted on a horse. The horses themselves wore armour shaped to the head, neck and body.

Weapons used during the 14th Century such as the sword, lance or arrow, could find few openings in plate armour, but with the invention and gradual improvement of fire-arms it became less and less useful. It was discarded piece by piece until little remained except the helmet and breast plate, which continued to be worn by some mounted troops through the 19th Century. French cuirassiers wearing this protection went into action in 1914 and later in the same war every infantryman was issued with a steel helmet—but that starts another story.

6

TWENTIETH CENTURY CRAFTSMEN

Though armour as our forefathers knew it is no longer in use, many fine specimens still survive; and the craft and skills of the armourer are not entirely dead. One of the most interesting collections of arms and armour is to be seen in the Armouries in the Tower of London. Housed mainly in the White Tower, this collection originated in Henry VIII's Royal Armoury and workshop at Greenwich. This was later transferred to the Tower, and added to over the years.

The exhibits include many whole suits of armour, including those of several monarchs down to James II. Also on view are items presented to Henry VIII by the Emperor Maximilian. Armour was a common royal gift.

To maintain this splendid collection, a team of expert technicians is employed. Among their tasks are those of repairing or restoring defective exhibits, fashioning replacements for missing parts and making replicas. When a piece is withdrawn for repair, a replica is displayed in its place.

Naturally some use is made of modern science. Above we see craftsmen using oxyacetylene equipment in the making of a breast plate. But in general the tools as well as the skills of the trade remain the same as they have been for centuries. The picture on the left shows a rack of traditional armourer's tools still in use. They would have been equally familiar to an armourer of medieval times.

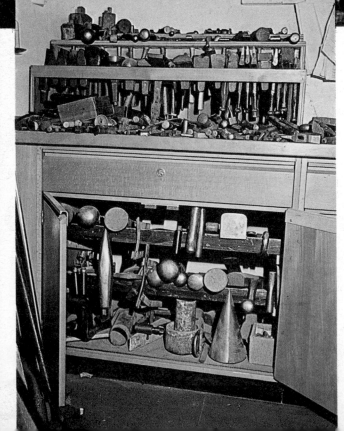

The Rescue of the Rumba

THUNDEROUS rumblings vibrated through the Norwegian freighter *Rumba* as it pounded among mountainous Atlantic waves.

On the bridge, Captain Elias Vaagnes clung to a rail as his swaying ship rose on the crest of a watery mountain before being dropped seconds later into a grey valley specked with foam.

Captain Vaagnes was groping for a 'phone when a huge wave smacked into the side of his ship with the force of an express train. Simultaneously, a giant drummer seemed to have gone mad in the ship's hold.

"The cargo!" the captain shouted to his first officer at the end of the 'phone. "What's happened to the cargo?"

Minutes later, he got his answer. It was to be the overture to one of the most dramatic rescue and salvage operations ever known.

It was just after midnight on 15th December, 1972. *Rumba* was 380 km. south-east of Newfoundland. She was bound for Yugoslavia with a cargo of 16 diesel locomotives, each weighing 116 tonnes. Eight were chained to the deck. Their bogies—the sections to which the wheels were fixed—had been taken off and chained securely at each end of the hold in which the other eight locomotives were being carried.

All went well when the *Rumba* set off from Toronto in Canada, through the St. Lawrence Seaway to the Atlantic where gales were already whipping up the sea fiercely. Such weather conditions are not uncommon in the Canadian winters, and Captain Vaagnes was not unduly worried in the circumstances. However, his alertness to possible danger began to be heightened when the increasingly unruly seas began tossing his ship around like a fragile toy in the hands of a clumsy giant.

Such conditions were tough for the crew, and they were especially murderous for the men faced with the havoc in the hold. Two of the locomotive bogies had broken loose from their moorings and were being thrown from one side of the hold to the other like huge roller skates. Risking their lives to do so, the men managed to get steel cables around the bogies and lash them safely in position.

But that was not the end of the trouble. *Rumba* sailed on, only to meet harsher and more tumultuous seas. Even bigger waves battered the ship, which felt to the crew as if it were being picked up, tossed from side to side and then left to fall into a boiling, foamy valley.

On top of the noise of the storm and the thunderous smashing of the seas against the side of the ship, there came more crashes and thuds from the hold. This time, they were so great that the ship vibrated with the force of them.

It was clear that the entire cargo was now being flung about in the hold. Hundreds of tons of iron and steel locomotives were skating from one side of the hold to the other. Time after time they were flung against the ship's side with unimaginable force. It was a miracle that they did not smash open the sides and send the ship diving helplessly to the ocean floor.

At the captain's order, all hands were sent to emergency stations, and the *Rumba's* radio officer began sending out a "Mayday" distress signal. Ships listening-in on the frequency picked it up and re-transmitted it to the Rescue Co-ordination Centres at Halifax, Nova Scotia, and New York.

A Canadian Argus aircraft was summoned from Prince Edward Island to locate the ship and send back radio reports about its predicament. Two hours later, a Buffalo turbo-prop went to join it. These could do little except drop rescue equipment and provide a radio link for the rescuers.

Meanwhile, help was on the way in the shape of the 812 tonne *Smit-Lloyd 103*, a supply boat whose normal job was to service and move oil drilling equipment. It had been at a rig 64 km. from *Rumba* when the distress signal had been received.

It reached *Rumba* at about 8 pm, when conditions were so bad that Captain Vaagnes ordered his men to abandon ship. Six men beat the furious ocean by getting aboard the *Smit-Lloyd 103* in a rubber raft, but this took about an hour and some of the men suffered from frostbite.

After he had seen how dangerous this operation was,

Captain Vaagnes refused to allow it to be repeated. A few hours later, a rescue helicopter arrived, but its crew could do nothing to help, so treacherous was the storm.

Meanwhile, the captain of the *Smit-Lloyd 103* was being faced with the problem of getting a towline attached to the *Rumba*. Daringly, in view of the very real danger of a collision, he got close enough to the *Rumba* to fire a harpoon-type gun with a line attached at the tossing ship's bows. But Rumba's crew were so badly storm-battered that they could not secure the line.

Tonnie Bakker, the *Smit-Lloyd's* first officer heroically solved the problem by jumping into a dinghy and letting it drift on the heaving ocean towards the *Rumba*. As he neared the freighter, eager hands lowered a rope ladder over the side for him to grasp. Once he was on board, another line was fired from the *Smit-Lloyd 103*. Bakker secured it and by 5.30 pm the rescue vessel was able to begin towing the *Rumba* towards the nearest port, St. John's, Newfoundland, 480 km. away.

When daylight came, the helicopter returned and lifted off the 13 remaining crew members as well as Bakker, leaving Captain Vaagnes in sole command of his crippled ship. Two nights without sleep lay ahead of him, on top of the sleepless hours he had endured during his ship's nightmare battering by the storm.

Gales even more treacherous than the one they had met before pounded the two vessels as they headed towards land. Half-a-mile of towing cable separated the two ships, invisible to each other in the darkness, but the skipper of the *Smit-Lloyd 103*, Captain Tjerk Straatman, a Dutchman, had to regulate his vessel's speed so that the cable remained taut and was neither slack nor strained. Had he allowed the cable to loop downwards in the sea, it could have become snagged by rocks and chopped in half. Had he pulled too powerfully on the cable he could have ripped away part of the freighter's bows.

Eventually, the pair made their way into the port of St. John's to the cheering of hundreds of people who had flocked to the harbour to see them.

An unforgettable rescue had been accomplished, one that would earn its place in the annals of sea history. But there was one flaw to this otherwise wholly successful achievement. On *Rumba's* deck were the empty spaces previously occupied by three of the eight locomotives she carried.

In the darkness of the storm-tossed night, they had broken loose and tumbled into the sea.

Bakker drifted towards the freighter where eager hands reached out to haul him aboard.

AIRPORTS FOR THE 80'S

With supersonic airliners comes the need for super efficient airports

THROUGHOUT the world international airports are reaching the limit to the number of planes and passengers they can handle. In New York, at peak times, delays of up to three hours are not unusual at both take-off and landing.

Soon, Sydney is likely to be only ten hours away from London. The growth of air transport will bring air travel within the reach of many more millions of people. In the next ten years it is estimated that passengers on the world's scheduled airlines could reach 1,000 million in a year. In Britain alone vast increases in the number of pass-

engers are forecast—by 1980 "the flying population" will be over 53 million a year, almost equal to our total population.

With Concorde in service, speeds have doubled to more than 2,090 km/h (1,300 mph). Today, normal cruising speeds are around 960 km/h (600 mph) the world's air speed record of 1949. It is quite clear that commercial aviation's most serious problem today is the continuous increase in air traffic.

One of the most important operations of an airport is to see that aircraft are up in the air and not on the ground. Modern airliners can cost many millions, and every

hour they are not airborne is money wasted. When an aeroplane lands it is methodically and quickly emptied, cleaned, serviced, refuelled and made ready for take-off. The average turn-round is from one-and-a-half to two hours.

There are more than 41,000 people working at London Airport, covering nearly every type of job—stewardesses, pilots, navigators, cleaners, engineers, chefs, waitresses, customs officers, police, doctors, nurses, firemen, radar operators—you name them, London Airport has them.

Heathrow (London) Airport originated in 1929 when it was known as Richard Fairey's Great West Aerodrome.

Since it became London's main airport in 1946, Heathrow has had to compromise because it was impossible to predict then how fast commercial aviation would expand. It is estimated that during the next ten years air passenger traffic will triple and air cargo traffic increase tenfold. To accommodate this new era of civil aviation London Airport, and every major airport in the world, will have to be replanned.

The six largest traffic centres in the world—Chicago, New York, Miami, Los Angeles, San Francisco and London—will eventually each require probably four major airports (each with four main runways) grouped around it to meet the requirements of the future. These Multiple-Airports would be placed so that nobody would have to travel too far to get to his nearest airport.

With such a pattern each of these major airports would be able to accommodate, without delays or congestion, approximately one million aircraft movements a year. That means perhaps 40 million passengers a year as a normal operation. So four airports would together provide comfortable capacity for four million aircraft movements and 160 million passengers a year. That is well ahead of demand, even in New York and Chicago up to the 1980s.

No airport should be more than thirty-five miles from a city centre. Surface journey times much in excess of forty-five minutes to and from airports are not acceptable in the supersonic era. An international airport handling 75 million passengers a year would need colossal road transport facilities, and it has been established that even with a city centre-airport transit system carrying 50% of the air passengers, the peak flow of road vehicles taking air travellers and airport employees to and from the airport might be 11,000 an hour. This volume of traffic would make it necessary to build 10 lane roads in each direction.

London's third airport has still to be chosen. The delay has been caused by opposition from communities to the siting of the airport because of destruction of beautiful scenery and farmland, as well as perhaps the biggest problem of all, aircraft noise. A new airport costs something like £100 million, and because of inflation the longer the delay the higher the cost. Many people believe that this money would be better spent on reclaiming land for a remote site. Others argue that it would be better spent on designing new engines or sound-proofing existing ones.

Short Take-off and Landing aircraft (S.T.O.L.) could be introduced in Britain within five years. British aircraft manufacturers think that vertical and short take-off planes carrying 100 to 200 passengers should be used to service routes of up to 800 km (500 miles). Plans for a 120 seat jet airliner that will take-off vertically and fly at 960 km/h (600 mph) have been announced by British Hawker-Siddeley. The H.S. 141 could enter service in the 1980s. It will have a range of 800 km (500 miles) or, if used for short-take off, it would have a range of 2,170 km (1,350 miles) and only need a 300 metre (1,000 foot) runway. Government experts predict that vertical take-off aircraft could carry 16 million passengers a year, using only a small corner of Heathrow Airport. All these various arguments have to be considered, and a decision for the international airports of the 1980s must be reached quickly.

The British Airports Authority has an unenviable task, but they look forward to the day—possibly before the year 2000—when passengers will be able to travel comfortably from any place on earth to any other in the space of a couple of hours.

If one looks back over the last 25 years of aviation nothing seems impossible.

The Hawker-Siddeley 141, seen here approaching Dallas Airport—one of the most modern in the world today—would be ideally suited for the requirements of airports of the future.

Short Take-off and Landing aircraft would enable airports to be constructed in the very heart of a city.

THE CLUES TO A LOST CIVILISATION

ARTHUR EVANS was a short-sighted coin collector who found a forgotten civilisation. Entirely by accident he discovered, at the beginning of this century, the remains of a magnificent city which dated back to 2000 B.C. It was the oldest city in Europe, and the birthplace of civilisation in the eastern Mediterranean.

He made his discovery on the island of Crete. The city he unearthed is Knossos, which was a thousand years old when the Greeks were clambering into their wooden horse at Troy.

It was a very upsetting find for many scholarly theories, for it proved that civilisation had not flowered first on the mainland of Greece as had been thought. The warrior cities of Greece, it seems, learned many of their cultured ways from earlier Knossos and other Cretan kingdoms.

As a young man, Evans travelled extensively in Eastern Europe and found time to study the ancient history of the countries through which he journeyed: he explored old ruins and collected coins, pottery and other artefacts.

About this time the German Schliemann discovered the ancient site of Troy, unearthing many fine relics.

This proved, without doubt, that Homer's epic poem of the siege was based on fact. The stories of ancient Greece were not, as had been thought, pure myth and legend.

When he was thirty-three, Evans was appointed Keeper of the Ashmolean Museum at Oxford—a task which allowed him great opportunity for travel.

In the course of his roamings he came upon some ancient small stones on sale in a market place in Athens.

The stones, or coins, were drilled as though for a thread and some of them had tiny markings. They were not in the familiar Greek letters but in some unknown hieroglyphs.

Being very short-sighted, Evans could see clearly tiny details on the coins which most people would need a magnifying glass to detect.

The dealer said the stones had come from Crete. Determined to solve the mystery, Evans set out for that island hoping to find some more of these stones and, if he was very lucky, to come across a clue to deciphering the writings.

Evans found plenty of the stones. The local women still wore them as lucky charms.

He noticed that there were numerous signs of ancient ruins on the island which he assumed to be old Greek settlements, until he began to dig. . . .

As he and his assistants probed into the Cretan soil, he found many hundreds of samples of the writings he sought. In addition, he unearthed walls, stairways, pavements, brightly-coloured frescoes depicting youths and maidens in garments very unlike those worn by Greeks or any other ancient people.

He found passageways which seemed to him like a maze. Was this the legendary maze of King Minos, who was supposed to have dwelt on Crete?

Images of bulls were found by the dozen, paintings were revealed of men and maidens performing the most extraordinary acrobatics on the backs of bulls.

Evans called to mind the story of Theseus, who entered the maze to slay the minotaur, a creature half man and half bull. Was this the city that gave rise to the legend at a time when the Greeks were, for the most part, still simple cottage-dwelling shepherds?

He discovered a great palace and a throne which he believed had belonged to King Minos. He gave the name "Minoan" to the brilliant and cultured civilisation he had found.

Evans worked at the site for many years, restoring the ruins to something like their original state, largely at his own expense. It is estimated that Knossos cost him a quarter of a million pounds.

Although some archeologists say that Evans did rather too extensive a job of restoration, his work certainly makes it possible for the ordinary visitor to imagine what Knossos must have been like in its heyday.

The throne room of King Minos at Knossos, with stone benches on either side and griffins decorating the walls.

The courts and buildings of Knossos cover an area of roughly six acres. On the left is shown the watch room of the palace.

Below: these huge earthenware jars were used for storage. Many of the treasures of Knossos have been removed and can now be seen in the museum in the town of Herakleion.

Above: the painted walls of the Queen's Apartment.
Below: the tapering columns of the Hall of Shields.

"One in the eye", could well be the title for this drawing by Lawson Wood—an artist who liked to get some fun out of pseudo-historical subjects.

They Made Grandad Laugh

...and Grandma too. In an age when there was often little cause for merriment, the cartoonists of the day brought a little laughter to the people of Britain.

A cartoonist at work: Lawson Wood, whose pictures, often dealing humorously with animals or historical subjects, won great popularity.

JOKES that appeal to one generation may not raise a smile 50 years later. But there are some comic artists whose humour never grows entirely stale.

The 30 years or so that covered the two World Wars and the years between were one of the richest periods in humorous art that this country has known. In fact the wars themselves inspired some of the finest examples.

Many of these artists had completed their training around the turn of the century, when more efficient methods of reproducing pictures was giving a boost to book and magazine illustration. Previously printing of pictures had been mainly done by means of wood engravings.

This generation of artists included men of such varied talents as Lawson Wood, Heath Robinson, Ernest Shepard and Frank Reynolds.

The magazine which many have thought to stand for the best, or at least the most typical, in pictorial humour is *Punch*. The fact is that, even after the First World War, it still retained something of its old Victorian and Edwardian flavour. Many of the jokes depended simply on the words accompanying the picture, which merely illustrated the incident related—much like an illustration in a book. In very few cases was the picture itself allowed to "tell" the joke, with or without the help of a brief caption.

Some of *Punch's* jokes at that time tended to be rather snobbish in the way they poked fun at humble folk. But some of its contributors, such as Bert Thomas or George Belcher, portrayed working-class characters with humorous sympathy that was quite free from snobbery.

Kenneth Bird, who worked under the name of Fougasse, was a star contributor to *Punch* for many years, and was eventually its Editor. After the Second World War he was to do much to change *Punch's* rather old-fashioned image. As an artist, Fougasse had a wonderful gift for conveying character and humour with a few deft strokes.

Another whose work often appeared in *Punch* was Lawson Wood. He had a highly individual style. He was a Fellow of the Royal Zoological Society; so it is hardly surprising that animals frequently featured in his pictures. He also liked to

DIG FOR VICTORY

CARELESS TALK COSTS LIVES

"..... but of course it *mustn't* go *any further*!"

HOW THE CAMOUFLAGE IDEA FIRST DAWNED ON THE MILITARY MIND.

Two World Wars gave cartoonists abundant scope both for light-hearted propaganda and for raising a laugh in otherwise cheerless times. Top left: Ernest Shepard, famed illustrator of the *Winnie-the-Pooh* books, calls amusing attention to the government's demands for more food production in 1940. Top right: the careless talkers in this poster by Fougasse are quite unaware of the presence in the luggage racks of the plump Nazi Marshal Goering and, presumably, Hitler himself! Above: a First World War cartoon by H. M. Bateman. Right: Bert Thomas catches the wry humour of the British Tommy in the trenches, in this 1917 sketch.

Tommy (back from Blighty). "YUS, I GRANT YER A BIT O' LEAVE 'S ALL RIGHT. BUT IT 'S AWFUL DEPRESSIN', TOO, AT HOME —NOTHIN' BUT WAR—WAR! IT GIVES YER THE FAIR 'UMP."

extract humour from pseudo-historical subjects.

An Australian-born artist whose work enjoyed great popularity between the wars was H. M. Bateman. Many of his cartoons depicted embarrassing situations. One of the best known was captioned "The guardsman who dropped his rifle..." The unfortunte soldier, caught in this nightmare predicament on a public parade, is shown as he would feel himself to be: a shrunken, cowering figure; while the other figures appear twice life-size, and bursting with eye-bulging indignation.

Ernest Shepard had a special gift for drawing appealing pictures of children—as in his *Winnie-the-Pooh* illustrations. Typical of his *Punch* cartoons about children is one in which a little girl is shown with her mother, who tells her to go to bed as she is "too young to stay up late." The child replies: "Well, that's your fault. You should have had me born sooner."

An artist with a manner and subject all his own was William Heath Robinson. Already established as an illustrator, he began to turn his hand to humorous drawing a few years before the First World War.

His name is especially associated with his pictures of complicated machines and devices, often made with knotted string and other primitive materials, and tended by solemn-looking little men. Today, over 30 years after the artist's death, his name is still used to describe any ramshackle contraption.

In both World Wars, Heath Robinson did his best to take people's minds off the grimness of the times with his pictures of ludicrous military devices, and with cartoons ridiculing the German foe.

Another artist based his humour on actual experience of warfare. This was Bruce Bairnsfather, who served as an officer on the Western Front in the 1914–18 war. He created the immortal character Old Bill, a soldier with a shaggy moustache, muffled in greatcoat and balaclava helmet. Old Bill became a famous figure, typifying the long-suffering private soldier of the British Army.

Bert Thomas was another serving soldier who put into his pictures the humour he found among the fighting men in the trenches. In war, as in peace, he was at his best in portraying down-to-earth men and women.

Newspapers as well as magazines have their comic artists. Some of these are political cartoonists, who express points of view about public affairs by means of their pictures. Some political cartoons are serious, but many rely on humour and caricature to make their point. One of the most successful newspaper cartoonists before and during the Second World War was David Low.

Another popular cartoonist was Sydney Strube, whose bowler-hatted "Little Man" stood for all the ordinary citizens who find themselves victims of the powerful people that run the world's affairs. The message of the Little Man cartoons is that all ordinary folk want is to get on with their own lives. It is a point of view well shown in a World War II picture, showing a wife in a garden air-raid shelter. To her husband (the Little Man), who has left the shelter, she calls: "Is it all right now, Henry?"— "Yes, not even scratched," is the Little Man's reply; and we see that all he is concerned with is his prize marrow, growing on top of the shelter.

An artist who set a new fashion in sports cartoons was Tom Webster. He had several imitators, though no completely successful rival in this field. He had a powerful talent for caricature. Many of the sporting figures he started as caricatures developed later into virtually fictional characters that constantly reappeared in his pictures.

A well-known heavyweight boxer of the day was on more than one occasion knocked out by foreign opponents. In Webster's cartoons he became a familiar character, as the Horizontal British Heavyweight— always on his back.

Those named here are only a few of the many able cartoonists of the period, whose work not only shows a wide range of artistic ability and a lively sense of humour, but also tells us much of the attitudes and way of life of the recent past.

Above: "Intelligent precautions" by leather-manufacturers to protect cattle hides—an example of the whimsical style of William Heath Robinson, whose caricature of himself (with his cat) appears on the right.

KEEPING IT COOL

THE domestic refrigerator is a simple, efficient device which, because it is so quiet in operation and relatively trouble free, we tend to take for granted. How does it work?

Firstly it is a compartment to hold food; therefore we make a large box with shelves. Secondly, it must be cold, so we remove all the heat. Finally, it must be insulated to ensure efficiency, so we put the box inside a larger one and pack the intervening space with an insulating material. Items all models have in common are the wire shelves, which allow the best possible air-circulation, and an exposed set of metal fins inside the cabinet.

The fins collect the heat from the inside of the compartment and take it outside; there it is dissipated in the surrounding air. If you put your hand at the back of an operating refrigerator, you can feel the warm air rising.

The insulation is to prevent additional heat from entering the compartment, for the essential scientific principle is that coldness is the *absence* of heat.

The fins rob the compartment of heat and energy, and thereby lower the temperature to a point at which the decaying process, from which all fresh foods suffer, is slowed right down.

The mechanism for removing the heat is remarkably straightforward, as the diagram shows.

Put simply, it is a continuous metal tube with a compressor/pump forcing along its length a liquid, usually freon or ammonia, which evaporates at a low temperature. Where the tube is narrow, the pressure and consequently the temperature is high. Where the circuit enters the refrigerator, the tube is widened, the temperature drops with the pressure, and the liquid becomes a freezing gas capable of absorbing the heat transmitted to it by the metal fins inside the refrigerator.

Wire shelves inside the fridge allow the air to circulate.

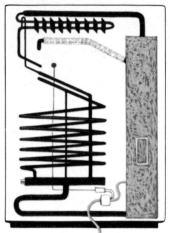

Above: the complex plumbing of the refrigerator and below the simple theory on which it operates.

REFRIGERATION – THE MODERN WAY TO TRANSPORT FOOD

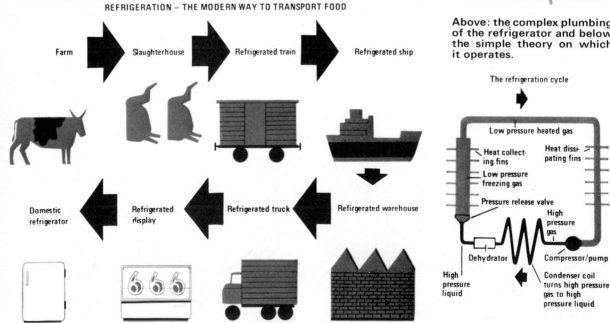

Farm → Slaughterhouse → Refrigerated train → Refrigerated ship

Domestic refrigerator ← Refrigerated display ← Refrigerated truck ← Refrigerated warehouse

The refrigeration cycle

Low pressure heated gas
Heat collecting fins
Heat dissipating fins
Low pressure freezing gas
Pressure release valve
High pressure gas
Dehydrator
Compressor/pump
High pressure liquid
Condenser coil turns high pressure gas to high pressure liquid

Butch's Wild Bunch

The photograph of Butch Cassidy's gang was the downfall of these robbers with a sense of humour.

INTO the Texas town of Fort Worth, still quite wild and woolly though the date was 1901, rode the three bank robbers. They were very pleasantly loaded down with the proceeds of their unexpected visit to the First National Bank at Winnemucca, Nevada, 32,640 dollars. They had far outstripped the sweating posse that had set out after them, being now a full thousand miles from the scene of their latest crime. It was time for the cream of the Wild Bunch, their leader, Butch Cassidy, his particular pal, the Sundance Kid, and that virtuoso villain, Bill Carver, to relax. The greatest outlaw gang in the last years of the Wild West had done it again.

A celebration was called for, especially when the unholy trio found that two more of the boys were in town, Harvey Logan, the one really bad man in the Bunch, and Ben –the Tall Texan–Kilpatrick. It was time to discard their trail gear, hang up their Stetsons and have a bath, especially Bill Carver, who had come off second best in an encounter with a skunk back at Winnemucca. While the robbery was in progress, the bank clerks could hardly bear to hold up their hands high so badly did they want to hold their noses!

After bath time, the boys climbed into new clothes, and new clothes, even for rugged Westerners on the spree, usually meant the height of Victorian fashion, natty gents outfits, derbies (bowler hats) included.

Now the five headed for the photographic saloon and sat there like a group of businessmen, which was what they considered they were. Hadn't they founded the Train Robbers' Syndicate? Even the James boys had never thought of doing that in their train-robbing days. And when they had had their famous photo taken–a mistake as it turned out–they even found time to take up the latest craze that had just hit the West, bicycling. Bicycling bandits? Readers will be getting the message, for these were bad men with a difference, and much of that was due to their leader, the cheerful, likeable Butch Cassidy, the crack shot who had never killed a man and didn't intend to start.

But before looking at the Frontier freak who didn't kill, a word more must be said about that picture. The proud photographer who took it gave an extra copy of it to Butch, who sent it off to the bank manager of Winnemucca to thank him for contributing to their fortunes. That is the sort of thing that Butch did. It hangs there to this day. Meanwhile, back in Fort Worth, and not long after the boys had moved out, a Wells Fargo detective spotted the photo hanging up in a place of honour and recognised Bill Carver. His bosses recognised the rest. Pinkerton's detectives, the leading crime-busting crusaders in the West, were glad of the perfect picture, and so were Union Pacific lawmen, whose railroad had given the boys so much illegal pleasure. The hunt for them was now on.

Which is a good moment to meet the man most wanted by the assorted lawmen, Butch Cassidy. His real name was Robert (not George, which some books allege) LeRoy Parker and we are happy to reveal that he was–almost–British to the backbone. No wonder he was likened to Robin Hood. Grandfather and father Parker came from Preston in Lancashire where, like many others in industrial Britain, they were converted to Mormonism and emigrated to America, crossing the Great Plains to the Mormon capital of Salt Lake City, pushing their belongings in a handcart.

Robert was born in 1866, growing up more interested in Mike Cassidy than in Mormonism. Mike ran a tough bunch of rustlers near the Parker homestead and took a liking to the strong, hero-worshipping boy, teaching him the arts of the cowboy and less respectable trades. It was in his hero's honour young Parker later took the name Cassidy. There are several explanations of the "Butch", one being that he worked for a while in a butcher's shop, another that he was knocked back by the recoil of a big gun, called Butch, into a waterhole.

He grew up in a period when the old open range was giving way to barbed wire, when small ranchers and settlers were "squatting" on land claimed by resentful cattle barons. When cattlemen, especially after savage winters, were learning modern methods, importing good stock from Britain, growing hay to feed their animals in winter, and needing less cowboys than before. This last, plus the tension between the cattle barons and the little men, led to more rustlers than ever, who became quite respectable in many eyes.

It came about that the loneliest parts of Wyoming and Utah were taken over by the rustlers, who even had two natural fortresses for protection, Hole-in-the-Wall, Wyoming, and Robbers Roost, Utah, both isolated and impregnable. A number of wild bunches sheltered in them, but by the late 1890s *the* Wild Bunch had been formèd, which varied in numbers, but whose hard core were the five we have met.

The Sundance Kid–real name Harry Longbaugh–was typical in that he had been cowboy, rustler and outlaw in that order. He was nicknamed for Sundance, Wyoming, where he once raised more than average hell. Unlike Butch, he was quite prepared to use guns to kill, but respected his friend's desire to keep the casualties to a minimum. Even Harvey Logan, dangerous and evil, respected Butch. The Bunch seemed to bare a charmed life, though once, in a surge of patriotism at the outbreak of the Spanish American War in 1898, they nearly spoiled

their record by riding in to volunteer. Fortunately, they suddenly remembered that nearly all of them except Butch were wanted for murder, so they went back to train-robbing.

On June 2, they halted the Union Pacific Overland Flyer at Wilcox, Wyoming, at 2.30 am by putting a red lantern on the track. They ordered the driver to detach the express car containing the money, then Cassidy touched off a stick of dynamite under it, strong enough to blow off one side, but not enough to kill the stubborn guard, one Woodcock, who was blown across the car. Logan typically wanted to kill him, but Butch said: "Let him alone. A man with his nerve deserves not to be shot."

But now Woodcock was hardly conscious, and was removed along with his gun. And then Butch blew the safe apart with more dynamite and thousands of dollar bills floated in the night air. The laughing outlaws gathered 30,000 dollars worth and vanished. Posses never got near them.

Incredibly, Woodcock was on duty again when the Wild Bunch held up a train at Tipton, and again behaved bravely until he realised that you couldn't argue with dynamite. But now the Law was out to get the gang. A special train was built with room for armed men and their horses, with orders to be ready to move any time night or day and to wipe out the Bunch. The six manhunters, equipped with special Winchesters and field-glasses, were a picked group, and when Butch heard about them, he decided that the days of train-robbing were nearly over.

So was their career after copies of the Fort Worth photograph had circulated the West. Butch and the Sundance Kid and the latter's pretty, sharp-shooting girl-friend, Etta Place, headed for New York–and more photographs–South America bound. There they had a marvellous time either working (occasionally) or robbing trains and banks. Etta, some say, had once been a schoolmistress. The official story is that the pair were finally killed in a giant shoot out with the Bolivian authorities, as depicted in that splendid film, *Butch Cassidy and the Sundance Kid*, by which time Etta had returned to the States. But it has finally been proved that the boys were not at that gunfight and that they returned home to live incognito, Butch dying in 1937, the Kid in 1957, both of old age.

Some readers will reasonably shout: "Rubbish!" at those words, knowing only too well that most of the stories of the famous who didn't die–Joan of Arc, Jesse James etc.–are pure invention or wishful thinking. This is almost certainly a rare case of survival. Butch's sister, the 13th and youngest of the Parkers recalled the day that Butch arrived home in a Model T Ford sixteen years after he and the Sundance Kid had "died" in 1909. Most of his gang had met violent deaths or been thrown into prison long before. Butch's sister wrote a book about it all, which was a sensation in America, as well it might be. The only really likeable rogue in the West and his by no means unlikeable friend got away with it.

So determined was the law to put an end to the escapades of the Wild Bunch, that a special train was built to carry armed men and their horses. Their orders were simple—be ready, night or day, to set of in pursuit of the robbers.

ONE of the weapons that causes headaches for naval vessels in wartime is the sea mine. During World War II hundreds of vessels of all kinds, both naval and mercantile, were sunk or severely damaged by these powerful underwater weapons.

A number of different trigger mechanisms are fitted to mines, any one of which can cause them to detonate. They can be set off by the magnetic field generated by the metal bulk of a ship passing over them; vibration waves set up by the ships' propellers can also trigger off a mine, and the sound of its throbbing engines (sound waves carry well under water) may also trip the firing mechanism.

In addition to these hazards, ships had also to face the possibility of actually striking a mine moored just below the surface in shallower waters. Apart from these trigger mechanisms, it is more than likely that present day mines have even more sophisticated devices fitted to them, making the problem of avoiding them even more difficult and dangerous.

Although the magnetic trigger was counteracted during World War II by fitting ships with what was called 'de-gaussing' equipment which neutralised their magnetic field, no satisfactory solution was found to the sonic and vibration sensitive triggers. The best way to deal with the mine menace was to remove them by 'sweeping'.

The task of sweeping for mines is, of course, carried out by the Royal Navy, and although methods used during World War II were quite effective, the mine-sweepers and their crews were exposed to considerable danger. Even though a sharp look-out was maintained for floating mines in known minefields, there was always the possibility of even a shallow draught vessel striking one, or setting one off with the sound of its engines.

Today, thanks to the invention of the hovercraft, the Navy will soon have a new and safer vessel to use for mine counter-measures. From the Navy's point of view, hovercraft have one big advantage over normal surface vessels–they travel on a cushion of air, and their hull is therefore actually out of the water. This gives them what is described as low noise, magnetic and pressure signatures, and makes them almost totally immune from damage due to underwater explosions–a great advantage when working over a minefield.

One of the latest, (and largest) hovercraft built for possible use by the Royal Navy is the VT-2 built by the British firm of Vosper Thorneycraft. The Navy already has a number of hovercraft, but none so large as the

ANSWER TO THE

VT-2 which has a length of 30 metres (99 ft), a breadth of 13 metres (43½ ft), weighs 60,960 kilos (60 tons) empty and nearly 101,600 kilos (100 tons) fully loaded.

The VT-2 can be adapted for use in a number of roles –a logistic support or supply vessel, a fast missile craft capable of carrying a modern automatic 3-inch gun and guided missiles, and for operation as a mine countermeasure vessel.

The propulsion units of this powerful new hovercraft are two Rolls-Royce Proteus gas turbine engines developing 3400bhp each, and they drive two ducted fans with variable pitch blades for controlling thrust and manoeuvring. The large size of the fans makes possible low noise at the tips of the blades and so reduces the overall noise level which is so important when dealing with sensitive acoustic mines.

The VT-2 can operate at speeds of over 60 knots (107 Km.— 67mph+) and it has been designed to operate over sand, mud flats, shallows, and debris strewn water. It will also clear five-foot obstacles and it is tough enough to take a considerable amount of damage to its skirt and superstructure from small arms fire without losing performance.

The deep air-cushion of the VT-2 gives it excellent sea-keeping qualities and a smooth ride, and it has a range which enables it to reach all countries who are members of the North Atlantic Treaty Organisation, and it can also be transported by ship if it is needed to operate in more distant waters.

The cargo deck can accommodate loads up to 513 kilos (32 tons), such as heavy guns, light tanks and scout cars, or 130 men with their equipment and vehicles.

MINE MENACE ?

Tim

AUGUST 5,1914

BRITA

AT

WA

DELIVER THE GOODS.

In this 1915 cartoon, Lloyd George is shown as Minister of Munitions.

THE FIGHTER WHO WANTED PEACE

IT was 1901. A solitary figure wearing an overcoat and peaked cap that was totally unlike his public image, walked through the angry crowds that thronged the streets close to Birmingham Town Hall. When it had been announced that he was to speak at a public meeting, men had talked of lynching him. The seriousness of their hate against him could also be borne out by the number of people who carried bricks and dangerous chemicals to throw at him when he arrived at the Hall.

The man who was to be their target that evening–the man in the peaked cap and borrowed overcoat– was none other than the legendary David Lloyd George: the man who sixteen years later, was to become prime minister of England and the man who, many people believe, was the principal figure in ending the war against Germany between 1914 and 1918.

Why then was there such terrible rancour against this man at the turn of the century? What he had done might have been forgivable in some parts of the country, but,

Many people believe that Lloyd George played a major part in bringing the 1914–18 war to an end.

Lloyd George loved to meet the people and is seen here at an open-air political rally.

In 1922 Lloyd George played a famous game of golf during which he and the French Premier Briand, worked out a settlement following the 1914–18 war with Germany.

A statesman of international standing, Lloyd George is seen here with French Premier Clemenceau (left) and Woodrow Wilson the US President.

according to the people of Birmingham, he had committed high treason. He had declared himself to be against the South African war, which is known more familiarly as the Boer War. As a pacifist he condemned it not only for its cost in human life but in money. His speeches branded him as "pro Boer", a friend of the "enemy", merely because he regarded it as a senseless butchery of both Englishmen and their foe, the Dutch settlers whose territory was rich in gold. It was a war of greed and Lloyd George did not mince his words when declaring himself against it.

In Birmingham he went against all advice to dissuade him from appearing in public. He refused to have one single bodyguard and decided instead that the best thing for him to do was mingle with the very crowds who had come to do him harm. And, what is more, his plan worked. He made his way, alone, through thousands of demonstrators and arrived safely on the public platform inside the town hall.

Unfortunately the only people

who heard his speech were the reporters to whom he dictated it. It was impossible to do otherwise in a city where the most respected citizen was Joseph Chamberlain, the Colonial Secretary, a prominent advocate of the war in South Africa.

The town hall door was battered down by the angry mob, the police cordons were swept away and eventually 7,000 people were jammed inside fighting either like wild animals or trying to save themselves from being crushed to death. Lloyd George sought refuge in an adjoining committee room and from there, disguised as a policeman, he dodged to safety via a back door into the snow-swept street.

In that riot, one man was killed, ninety-seven police were injured, forty people were detained in hospital and more than a thousand windows were broken.

Had Lloyd George not escaped the crowd that stormy night–and he might well have been the victim of a bullet, for shots *were* fired– England would have been deprived of one of its greatest statesmen.

He was a man of tremendous wit and imagery, a brilliant orator, a humanitarian and a man of considerable courage.

What makes such a man?

His father, a schoolmaster who suffered from ill-health, died before he was a year old and he was educated at the National Church school in Llanystumdwy, a village in north Wales.

Lloyd George was born in Manchester on January 17, 1863 and his family moved to a farm in Pembrokeshire soon afterwards. When his father died his uncle, Richard Lloyd, responded at once to the simply worded telegram from David's mother "Come Richard". He walked twenty miles to the nearest railway station, travelled by train to south Wales where he picked up baby David, his mother and his brother, and took them back north to his five-roomed

Criccieth, were Lloyd George had his flourishing law practice.

WOMEN WIN THE RIGH[T]

DAILY SK[ETCH]
THE PREMIER PICTURE

Six Million
Women Can Vote
VOTES FOR WOMEN PAS[S]

Many Peeresses Listen to
Grave Warnings.
MAJORITY OF 63.

"Hurrah! It's a fine ending to a long
fight."
    This exclamation was made over the tele-
phone by an official of the Women's Party
when told of the House of Lords's decision
last night on Lord Loreburn's amendment to
the Reform Bill to omit the clauses giving
the vote to 6,000,000 women.
The division resulted as follows:—

Woman she[
Lord
The division w[
and amidst muc[h
keenly interested

DELICATE

Refused to Eat

cottage.

"Uncle Lloyd" as Richard was known from then on, devoted his life to caring for the family. He was a shoe-maker but there was nothing ordinary about him. He, more than anyone else was responsible for David's progress in his formative years. In addition to being a shoemaker he was a Baptist lay preacher and a student of philosophy.

David did not agree wholeheartedly with his uncle's strict religious beliefs. In fact, he became an earnest noncomformist at quite an early age. But he read the Bible voraciously because he considered there was nothing like a theological argument to sharpen the wits.

That a boy should aspire to become a lawyer in any circumstance is to aim high, but for him to do so when he is attending a village school which has a curriculum limited to reading, writing and arithmetic, and occasional lessons in History and Geography, is to aim almost for the unattainable. Yet Lloyd George qualified as a solicitor at the age of twenty one.

Lloyd George's law firm in Criccieth on the coast at Tremadog Bay in north Wales became famous;

Two major political events in Lloyd George's career were the granting of the vote to women in 1918 and, in 1922, the creating of a free state in Southern Ireland. Then, as now, Ireland was a country torn by strife with the use of firearms and violence an everyday occurrence.

he went into court battles like a tornado and even went so far as to question a magistrate's abilities on one occasion.

At the age of 25 such was his reputation that he was elected an alderman; two years later he became the Liberal M.P. for Caernarvon Boroughs in a celebrated by-election that was "rigged" against him. Twenty votes "for" him were deliberately placed amongst those in favour of his opponent. They were discovered in a recount and Lloyd George came out the winner by a mere eighteen votes: the poor boy from a humble home had beaten the local squire.

From then on the name of Lloyd George was to become known to the world. In 1905 he was appointed President of the Board of Trade; in 1908, Chancellor of the Exchequer; and in 1916, Prime Minister. But his greatest achievement was trig-

gered off, curiously, when he personally took part in a hunt for Jack the Ripper, the psychopathic killer who was terrorising the East End of London. The search took him through one of the worst slum regions in the world; so bad were the conditions that one could have been excused for suggesting that the Ripper—who was never found—was performing acts of mercy and not fearful murder. Lloyd George later wrote: "I set out to investigate a crime that night; I found evidence of ten thousand."

From that night he campaigned against poverty and in 1911 his work bore fruit: the National Insurance Act was passed which was to attack poverty caused by illness and unemployment by a system of compulsory insurance.

For fifty years Lloyd George continued to raise his voice on the small as well as great issues, but in 1944 he left his Surrey home and returned to the very place he had known as a boy—to Llanystumdwy, in north Wales and in January the following year he became Earl Lloyd-George of Dwyfor. Although he died three months later, the impact of his political contributions will always be felt.

TWENTY DAYS IN THE HUT OF HORROR

Thanks to a group of heroic volunteers and the dedication of an army doctor, yellow fever - the scourge of the tropics - has been tamed.

THE living tomb was ready. It was a nasty, airless little "house", 4.2×6m (14×20ft), with a stove blazing away to keep the temperature well over the 90 mark.

Beside the stove were tubs of water, which helped make the atmosphere like a particularly steamy Turkish Bath. When everyone was satisfied that a tropical inferno had been created and that no draught could get in from outside, sol- diers carried sinister-looking, nailed up boxes into the room and put them on the floor.

Soon after the soldiers left, sweating and cursing, three Americans entered the swelter- ing room. They were young Doctor Cooke and two soldiers named Folk and Jernegan. Then the door was shut.

It was now time to open those boxes.

Out came stinking pillows, soiled with the sickness of men dead from that scourge of the

The volunteers unpacked the grisly contents of the boxes.

Tropics–Yellow Fever. Next came blankets and sheets in which the dying had lain. The trio made up their beds with these grisly relics and tried to sleep in the nightmare chamber.

If the "experts" were right, they would soon be dead, but a few men, also experts, led by a United States Army Doctor, Major Walter Reed, believed that they would live.

Against all evidence Reed was convinced that mosquitoes, and only mosquitoes, could give a man Yellow Fever, or Yellow Jack as it was commonly called. The year was 1900, the place Cuba, where the Americans had been fighting the Spaniards, and losing thousands more men to the dreaded disease than ever Spanish bullets killed. No mosquitoes could get into Reed's specially built hell hole. If the three men did not get the fever, he would have surely proved his point.

The three were sent in food, also more boxes filled with filth from diseased victims. Then, after 20 endless days, they were let out and put into quarantine. Had they got Yellow Fever? They had not!

Walter Reed tried again. He sent three more heroes in, this time to sleep on pillows specially decorated with towels bathed in the blood of the dead!

They, too, survived. Then came the greatest test of all. . . .

THE BEGINNING

But before revealing the final horror, we must go back to the beginning of this grimmest of bug-hunting sagas.

For centuries Yellow Fever had cursed parts of Africa, the West Indies and the Americas. It got its name because its wretched victims literally go yellow. Its most horrible symptom is that the patient vomits "black blood". In some of the worst outbreaks, 85 per cent of those who caught the horrible plague died.

Before the cause was realised, stark panic would hit towns where Yellow Jack broke out. Curtains and seat covers, houses even, were burnt, and those who had not caught the disease left town and did not return until the outbreak had died down. In the southern United States this meant waiting until the autumn.

It was this appalling scourge that Walter Reed, born in 1851, and a man who had seen service in the Wild West and elsewhere, set out to combat.

Everyone was in despair when he reached Cuba and set up his four man Yellow Fever Commission. Everyone that is except a friendly old doctor, Carlos Finlay, who had a quaint idea that the mosquito was the villain of the piece. Naturally, everybody laughed at him.

But Walter Reed was prepared to listen to anyone and he met Finlay. He also noticed an interesting fact, that nurses dealing with Yellow Jack victims rarely got the disease. Why not? Perhaps because they rarely met with swamp mosquitoes.

So he started his deadly tests, naturally using only volunteers. The first tests were simple: a mosquito was put on a healthy man and proceeded to bite him!

The first volunteer to get infected nearly died, but Reed could not consider that to be proof, and even when one man did die, it did not prove that he had not got the disease already. Reed himself wanted to "take the bite", but his colleagues would not let him, especially as he was 50. But he did get permission to pay his volunteers properly, even though they might not live to spend the money.

Proof kept piling up, but still the experts sneered, and it was at this point that Reed had the nightmare hut built.

We left our heroes waiting for a final test, and when it came it might well have been final! Jernegan had evil Yellow Fever blood shot under his skin and Folk was bitten with mosquitoes which had feasted on

After 20 days inside the hut the men were released.
Now came the anxious days of waiting . . .

Canal by exterminating the mosquitoes of the Panamanian swamps.

But there were still some "experts" who doubted. Reed once had some of them in his laboratory, where he knocked over a bottle containing mosquitoes, and watched the doubters rushing from the room. As it happened these were "clean" mosquitoes.

ANOTHER VILLAIN

That is not quite the end of the story, for years later it was found that the swamp mosquito living near man is not the only villain. Another species, which lives in forests can also transmit the disease, without first feasting off a man, and you cannot destroy forests in the way you can clean up swamps!

Scientists finally found a vaccine to give short term immunisation from the disease, which is why, before going to certain countries, travellers are immunised. So, one type of Yellow Fever has been wiped out in many countries, the other has been tamed. The vaccine used is 100 per cent effective. Reed and his valiant volunteers, all of them dead now – mostly of old age – did not strive in vain.

fatal cases. Both got Yellow Jack and both survived – just.

Reed had been forced to carry out this final horror because the experts were liable to claim that the two men were immune to the disease, so could survive the hut. As the two went straight down after the final tests, these tests showed that mosquitoes, not clothing etc. must be the culprits.

Finally, after more tests, Reed proved beyond all doubt that the villains were mosquitoes who had already bitten Yellow Fever victims, then transmitted the virus to others.

If Yellow Fever was discovered, whole houses and their contents were burnt in an effort to destroy the disease.

SPEEDY ACTION

At once, some people took action. Typical was Dr. William Gorgas who cleared Havana in Cuba of Yellow Jack in 90 days by destroying all the mosquitoes in cisterns, cesspools and elsewhere. For the first time in 200 years the city was free of the disease. Gorgas later made it possible to build the Panama

Was the mosquito the cause of the fever? The simplest way to find out was to put one on a healthy man and let it take a bite!

A general knowledge quiz to test your wits.

Ask Me Another

1. In which state of the USA are the Adirondack Mountains?
2. What do the initials UNESCO stand for?
3. In which year did Queen Victoria open the Great Exhibition—an Exhibition of the Works of Industry of all Nations?
4. The Crystal Palace was built especially for the Exhibition and, when it was over, was moved to a new site in South London. When did Queen Victoria re-open the Crystal Palace on its new site?
5. On a cold night in 1936 the Crystal Palace was destroyed. How?
6. At 7.55 a.m. on 7th December, 1941, an event took place which precipitated the United States into the Second World War. What was it?
7. Which king of England was born at Oxford on 24th December 1167?
8. Sarah Siddons made her first appearance at Drury Lane Theatre on 29th December, 1775. What was her role?
9. Who discovered that the element uranium continually emitted invisible radiations which could affect a photographic plate.
10. Who was the first Astronomer Royal?
11. Who founded the newspaper, "The Daily Mail"?
12. What is the capital of Norway?
13. Who wrote the novel "The Picture of Dorian Gray"?
14. Which famous British actress died in October, 1976? Among the many roles she played were those of Millamant in "The Way of the World" and Lady Bracknell in "The Importance of being Earnest"?
15. Who was the first king of Italy?
16. What name is given to the room attached to a church in which the vestments are kept?
17. Gardeners regard the ladybird as a friend. Why?
18. What are the three main differences between a frog and a toad?

NOW TURN TO PAGE 127 FOR THE ANSWERS

Thank You, Aunt Emma!

When Emma Cons summoned her niece to return home from South Africa, she could not have known that the young girl was destined to become a legend in the British theatre.

Never one to mince her words, Lilian Baylis told Queen Mary just what she thought of her late arrival.

"I'M glad you've turned up at last, dear," said the short dumpy woman with the crooked mouth to Queen Mary, grandmother of our present Queen. After all, it was the centenary performance of London's famous Old Vic Theatre, and its manager was not one to mince her words.

"I know it's not your fault being late," she continued, "as I hear that your Dear Husband going to the Union Jack Club has held up the road. But we've got a long programme to get through and had made a start. So let's get on with things!"

The Queen of England rapidly took her seat.

The Manager's name was Lilian Baylis (1874–1937), an astonishing woman who made her theatre great and created not one but three national theatres. Today, the Royal Ballet, the English National Opera and the National Theatre are renowned throughout the world, but it is safe to say that none of them would exist, certainly not in their present form, if it had not been for Lilian Baylis.

She was a woman of little education, much religious faith and indomitable spirit, who would pray to God for "good actors and cheap", not because, as some alleged, she was mean, but because it was all her theatre could afford. In her day there were no state subsidies for the arts in Britain. She begged, prayed and cajoled and she managed to collect some of the finest actors in the country to work for her at far less than they got elsewhere. Their names included Laurence Olivier, Sybil Thorndike, Ralph Richardson, Peggy Ashcroft, John Gielgud, Edith Evans and many more.

She was a Londoner and her first talent was for music, making a name for herself as a child prodigy on the violin. In 1891 she and her family went to South Africa and were soon entertaining miners after they had finished looking for gold in the daytimes. Lilian was billed as "Soprano, Vocalist, Violinist and acknowledged premier lady Mandolinist and Banjoist of South Africa".

While not astounding the locals with her versatility, she used to enjoy swimming, but once got into difficulties. Wave after wave battered her face on one side and she fainted. She was rescued, but woke to find that side of her face crooked. Gradually it recovered, except for her mouth, which remained crooked for life.

Then Fate summoned her to England, or, rather, her Aunt Emma did, thus changing the course of theatre, operatic and balletic history. Aunt Emma, known to the public as Emma Cons, was a typically Victorian do-gooder of the best sort, in other words she got things done. In her case it was the transformation of the Old Vic Theatre.

This had originally opened in 1818 as a major playhouse, but by 1879 it had become so disreputable that it had had to be closed. The next year Miss Cons reopened it for the sober "deserving poor" as the Royal Victorian Coffee Music Hall. In 1898 Lilian Baylis took over the day-to-day running of the theatre and began her life's work.

First money had to be raised and she had soon added the new-fangled silent motion pictures to the theatre's attractions. Cinemas were to steal her thunder, but enough was raised to help promote concerts, then opera in English. By 1914, two years after Aunt Emma died, the work of Shakespeare was performed at the Old Vic.

The theatre was hopelessly cramped backstage, especially now that two companies were sharing it, and money was desperately short. Scenery was often not just simple but primitive. But enthusiasm was intense behind and in front of the curtain. This was a People's Theatre visited by men, women and children of all classes. Even the poorest could afford a two-penny seat in the gallery (from which Miss Baylis was quite prepared to eject a drunk herself) and the best stalls were only a shilling at that time, perhaps less than £1 by today's reckoning. And from the first major talents were drawn to the Old Vic, despite the tiny salaries, one of them being the young Sybil Thorndike, who during the First World War—and consequent shortage of men—often found herself playing male as well as female roles.

Lilian Baylis never let up in the search for money and regularly prayed for aid. The Old Vic was so often saved from what seemed to be ruin that some believed "The Lady", as she was called, had God on the staff. Meanwhile, for relaxation she swam, went for picnics and took up driving, her speciality being that she never stopped the car once she had started, considering signals beneath her notice. Somehow she survived—like the Old Vic.

By 1930, when John Gielgud first played at the Vic, the theatre was already world famous, though still short of funds, and in 1931 Lilian Baylis, having raised yet more funds by her usual methods, added a second theatre to her empire, reopening a totally rebuilt theatre in Islington, Sadler's Wells. At first drama and opera were given at both theatres, but soon the drama was confined to the Old Vic and the

The Old Vic Theatre.

Sadler's Wells Theatre, reopened by Lilian Baylis.

Above centre: Laurence Olivier and Sybil Thorndike in *Coriolanus*. Right: Olivier as Richard III.

Without Lilian Baylis we would not have the Royal Ballet, now at Covent Garden (below centre) or the English National Opera at the Coliseum (below).

The National Theatre.

opera to the Wells. And in 1932, the Sadler's Wells Ballet came into being, which years later was to become the Royal Ballet, just as the Sadler's Wells Opera finally (at the Coliseum) became the English National Opera.

Lilian Baylis had a genius for selecting the right people, among them Ninette de Valois, the first artistic director of the ballet company. Before the company was formed the dancers had merely danced in those operas that included a ballet, now they were equal in status with the others. Early stars included one still dancing today, Margot Fonteyn.

Even Lilian Baylis could not go on forever, despite her tremendous strength of mind, body and spirit. The strain was beginning to tell. By the mid-

Lilian Baylis thought nothing of ejecting a drunk from the gallery of her beloved Old Vic.

1930s she was one of the most famous women in Britain and was regarded with awe. She had her enemies, for she was very outspoken, and some resented her apparent meanness because they failed to grasp that it was not her money at stake but the Old Vic's and Sadlers Wells's money–and there was still not enough of it. She was equally proud of both theatres. Once, when knocked down in the street, she was recognised by a worried bystander who said: "Why, it's Miss Baylis of the Old Vic!" Lilian Baylis opened her eyes and said: "And Sadler's Wells!"

In November 1937, her beloved pet dog was run over, then the

first night of *Macbeth* (starring the young, but already famous, Laurence Olivier) had to be postponed, something that had never happened in the whole history of the Vic. Lilian felt she had failed her beloved public. These events, plus years of overwork, led to her death on November 25, when her valiant heart finally ceased to beat. But her three companies were safe now and were to survive the Second World War.

In 1974 her centenary was celebrated at the Old Vic Theatre and elsewhere, an Old Vic which housed an official National Theatre. Lilian Baylis's name was recalled with love, affection and awe. She had founded three national theatres, this strange, often impossible, marvellously single-minded woman of genius.

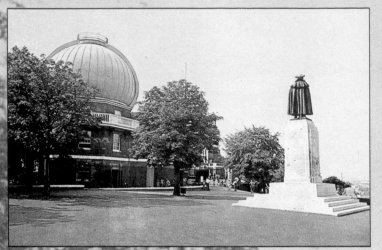

Designed by Christopher Wren, the Royal Observatory (above) was founded in 1675. Now open as a museum, it houses a fine exhibition of historical astronomy. Running through its courtyard (right) is the prime meridian, from which all other longitudes are measured.

Greenwich
Time Centre of the World

FOR its historical associations it must be among the richest in Britain. It was the birthplace of Henry VIII and the setting for his marriage to Catherine of Aragon. Both Charles I and Cromwell lived there during their respective periods in history and an early saint, Alphege, was martyred there by the Danes in 1012.

All these are epoch-making events, but it is for none of these things that a borough on the edge of London is so famous that its name rings around the world at regular intervals every day.

The borough is Greenwich, renowned in every quarter of our planet where maps are read and clocks are used. Its fame is based

Stand astride the brass strip, which marks zero longitude (far left) and you can have one foot in the eastern hemisphere and the other in the west. Outside Flamsteed House, named after the first astronomer royal, John Flamsteed, stands this clock. Beneath it is a plaque which states that it shows Greenwich Mean Time, the basis of the international time zone system.

upon a narrow brass strip that runs across a cobbled courtyard. This strip marks zero longitude; this is drawn on maps as a huge circle which divides the Earth from north to south, passing through the north and south poles. All other longitudes are measured from here in angles. And time is calculated from this point, too, for all other nations describe their time as being so much in advance of, or behind, Greenwich time.

Greenwich has this particular distinction because England in the past led the world in both astronomy and navigation. The building outside which the zero longitude strip—or meridian—lies is Flam-steed House, named after John Flamsteed, who was appointed the king's astronomer in 1675. In that same year, the building of Greenwich Observatory was begun and Flamsteed moved into it as soon as it was finished. Flamsteed's great work was in cataloguing the fixed stars, for these were like signposts in the sky to the early navigators. But to find their ship's position at sea, the navigators needed to know two things. First, it was necessary to ascertain their own local time, which was measured from the sun or the stars. It was also essential to have Greenwich Mean Time.

Local time is determined with a sextant, which measures the height of the sun, moon or stars above the horizon. This measurement is then used for calculating local time by looking up the position of the stars in a Nautical Almanac. This lists the places of the stars, moon and sun for every hour at every latitude. As the position of the stars is known from the sextant, and the latitude as well, local time can be quickly determined.

The local time is then compared with Greenwich Mean Time and the longitude is then calculated. Today, of course, radio is used to position a ship at sea, but every navigator has to learn how to calculate longitude by using a sextant and Greenwich Mean Time, in case the radio should suddenly go dead.

Nowadays, Greenwich Mean Time is provided by radio. But two hundred years ago there was neither radio nor an accurate clock to make this possible. Things became so desperate that governments were offering huge sums of money for a clock that would keep time at sea. In 1714, the British government offered £10,000 for a clock that would stay accurate enough to measure longitude (the distance from Greenwich) to one degree on a voyage to the West Indies and back again.

A master clock-maker, called John Harrison, devoted all his energy to making an accurate clock. He eventually sent one on a voyage to Spain and back with great success, but the government refused to award him their prize money because the clock was so accurate that they thought it was a trick. It was not given to him until he was old and dying. By then he had proved his chronometers—as accurate clocks are called—time and time again, on many voyages and in varied conditions. Eventually, a clock based on Harrison's chronometer, was sent with Captain Cook to the Pacific in 1776.

Once accurate sea, or marine, chronometers were made, navigation became very much safer. The marine chronometer is set by Greenwich Mean Time when the ship leaves harbour, and this is used to assist in calculating a ship's position, as has already been described.

It is easy to see that great confusion would arise if the world abandoned the system of calculating its local time as being so many hours fast or slow of Greenwich. Because the Earth rotates from west to east around its axis, time varies from place to place. When the sun first appears over the horizon in London, people in New Delhi about 7,242 kilometres (4,500 miles) east of London, are already taking their midday rest, while in New York, 4,828 kilometres (3,000 miles) to the west, it is still night.

Even within a small island like Britain, people on the east coast see the dawn slightly earlier than people on the west coast. It would obviously be a nuisance if we had to alter our watches every five miles or so to adjust for local time as we travelled across the country. On the other hand, we do have to alter our watches if we travel great distances.

The only fully-rigged survivor of the 19th century clippers, the "Cutty Sark", built in 1869 and now open daily to visitors can be seen at Greenwich.

For convenience, the world has been divided into time zones, and all the places inside each zone keep to the same time. Each time zone differs from the next by one hour. Britain is small enough to fall within one time zone, Greenwich Mean Time. But America is much too big to have the same time across the width of its continent. There are, in fact, four time zones between the east and the west coasts, so that when you fly from Los Angeles to New York you save time!

If you travel eastwards in a ship from Britain you eventually come to a point, in the Pacific, where you are exactly 12 hours ahead of Greenwich time. This means that you see the dawn 12 hours before it is first seen in Greenwich. If you travel westwards, you would reach the same point in the Pacific, only you would be 12 hours behind Greenwich time.

Before the last century began, clocks in Britain were so many minutes fast or slow of Greenwich, and every town had its local time, from which the villages took theirs In a place like Plymouth, the town hall clock differed from the railway clock (which kept Greenwich time) by 15 minutes. Up to 1800, this confusion was general, then Greenwich Mean Time was made legal in Britain.

Since then, it has been general throughout the world, and an imaginary line has been drawn down the Pacific—the International Date Line—to show where the day begins so as to arrive at Greenwich precisely at noon. Time at this point is either 12 hours ahead of Greenwich or 12 hours behind it, depending upon the direction from which the line is approached.

The standard for Greenwich Mean Time was set in 1884 when an international agreement established that the meridian longitude should run through the Royal Observatory there. This guaranteed Greenwich Mean Time's worldwide acceptance.

Although London's polluted air forced the observatory to go to its present quarters at Hurstmonceux Castle in Sussex in 1958, the time that is winged constantly to all the nations on radio waves is still Greenwich Mean Time.

Today, it is recorded by silent quartz clocks that have outdated the earlier mechanical timepieces. Their accuracy is internationally famed, as is the place whose name they perpetuate. Such wide renown means that few tourists in London leave without making a river trip to Greenwich—the time centre of the world!

Behind the historic guns stands the entrance to the National Maritime Museum, which is the world's largest. Devoted to sea subjects, it is open daily. Admission is free but school parties should book in advance.

THE AMAZING CRAB

A LOOK AT ONE OF NATURE'S MARVELS

WHAT creature can taste with his legs, can grow a new eye if he loses one, can see ahead and sideways at the same time, has a dark-coloured shell by day and a lighter shade after dark? And, if an enemy grabs him by the claw, easily escapes by snapping off the captured leg at the joint?

The animal with these amazing attributes is the crab, of which there are 4,000 species. Most surprising of these is the crab's ability to grow a new leg.

A crab has ten legs. Each of these has a point selected by nature at which the leg can be snapped off without harming the crab. When a crab wishes to escape from a predator which has grabbed him by a limb, he makes his muscles tighten up so much around the breaking point that the captured part of the limb comes away from the rest of it. All the blood vessels are closed up to prevent the crab from bleeding to death and, in due course, a new leg starts to grow.

This is amazing enough, but the versatility of a crab's legs does not stop here. Scientists have discovered that there are taste buds in a crab's claws. They proved this by placing some paper soaked with meat juice on the bed of a crab's pool.

As soon as the crab's feet touched the paper, the animal sensed that it had something edible within its grasp–and began to feed.

It has this sense of survival instilled into it from the moment it begins life as one of many thousands of tiny eggs laid by its mother. Predators prey upon it from the time of its birth, and only the luckiest survive to pass through the various stages that begin with its arrival as a transparent dot in the ocean. After several months, it has evolved into a fully developed crab which will spend the rest of its life on the sea bed or in the warm pools at the shores.

Equipped with gills, the crab can breathe under water–or out of it. Protected by its tough shell, it can tunnel under rocks to seek a safe refuge from its enemies. It is helped in this endeavour by its ability to move an object many times its own weight.

The crab grows so swiftly in its first year that it sheds its shell frequently, each time revealing a brand new shining shell underneath. This is soft at first, and until it hardens the crab must remain in hiding, for a predator could easily make a meal of it at this stage.

As it advances into adulthood, the crab may make a startling discovery one day. After spending all its early life under the water, it could be washed on to a rocky shore by the receding tide and find a whole new world out of the water. In addition to realising that it can breathe on dry land, the crab may also find a swift method of locomotion–sideways running on moist rocks or soft sand.

What a remarkable amphibian the crab is! But there is still more to be known about this versatile creature. For instance, the shore crab will eat almost anything dead that it finds. Animals, birds, insects, the remains of somebody's picnic—they are all one to the crab, which cleans a shore of rotting refuse by eating it.

Here is another mystery. Some shore crabs have a strong sensing mechanism. Nobody knows exactly what this is, but it causes the pigmentation of the shell to change so that the crab has a lighter colour by night than it has by day. A crab's colouring is made up of three types of pigment. These are red, white and black, which cover its body in various combinations to make up a variety of shades.

When darkness falls, the crab's light-sensing mechanism causes these pigments to become smaller, and thus the shell's colour becomes lighter.

But of all the wonderful things a crab possesses, it would be hard to better its all-seeing eye, which rests protected for most of the time in a bony socket in the shell. When a crab wants to look around, it sticks out its eyes on the end of long stalks so that it can virtually look in any direction it wishes.

But an eye protruding on a stalk is very vulnerable to damage. So nature has given the crab an unbeatable spare parts service. If a hungry creature comes along, sees an eye on a stalk and gobbles it up, there is no need to worry. The crab simply takes a rest while a new eye grows.

Crabs vary in size from tiny "pea crabs" which live in the shells of oysters or mussels where they pay their rent by destroying organisms that might damage their host, to the giant spider crab of Japan which is frighteningly large. Incidentally, spider crabs are usually covered with dense growths of seaweed and sponges which have been planted by the crab itself and which form an effective disguise.

The hermit crab is a fascinating creature. In its early stages, it develops much like other salt water crabs. Later, it finds an empty shell to live in, adapting its body to fit the shell. When it gets too big for this shell, it swims off to find another.

Land crabs are found in tropical countries. The South Pacific islands are the home of the coconut crab, which is able to climb the coconut palm and gather its fruit. Certain species found in the West Indian Islands generally live three or four kilometres from the sea.

They are remarkable for their annual spring migrations to the sea, in which the females lay their eggs.

When the migratory instinct seizes them, they march in a huge army with the males in the lead.

Hills, houses, churches, cliffs—nothing stops them or turns them aside from their chosen route. The sea is their destination and absolutely nothing is going to stop them reaching it.

Remarkable? No more so than any of the other characteristics with which nature has endowed one of her most favoured creatures—the crab.

MAGNIFICENT REBEL

NAPOLEON called him "The Sea Wolf", while his South American opponents went one stage further and dubbed him "El Diablo", the Devil. He was a sailor in the Nelson class, a passionate politician and a far-sighted inventor. His name was Thomas Cochrane, and the reason that he is too often forgotten by his own country is that he dared to challenge Authority, or what today we call the Establishment.

Cochrane's crime was all the more unforgivable because in his own day the Establishment was so corrupt.

Born in 1775, the eldest son of the Earl of Dundonald, the young Cochrane went to sea in 1793, in the *Hind*, a frigate commanded by his uncle.

Young Cochrane proved a born sailor and born sailors were needed, for war had broken out with Revolutionary France. But for five years he found himself guarding fishing vessels off Newfoundland. However, 1798 saw him helping blockade Cadiz aboard *Barfleur*, based at Gibraltar.

One day he returned from a duck shoot ashore and rushed to change his filthy clothes before reporting to the First Lieutenant, Philip Beaver, who was furious at the delay. A row erupted and Cochrane challenged Beaver to a duel. The Admiral tried to calm the fire-eaters, but Beaver demanded a court-martial. Cochrane was severely reprimanded and told to be polite to his seniors in future.

Next, he was sent with dispatches to Torbay to the Fleet Flagship and was informed by the Flag Captain that he had broken quarantine regulations by coming aboard.

At last he saw action in the Mediterranean. He made a success of being given a barely seaworthy captured French ship, plus a crew of sick, wounded and malcontents, to sail to Minorca. He handled the task so well that he was rewarded with his first command, the sloop *Speedy*. In this 158-tonner armed with only fourteen 4-pounders, he captured 50 ships and 534 prisoners in a single year.

His most astounding feat was the capture of the Spanish frigate *El Gamo*. It had 319 men to Cochrane's 54 and could fire a broadside of 190 pounds to *Speedy's* 28. In 1801, he approached the Spaniard flying the American flag, then, ordering his men not to fire until they were alongside, raised the British ensign and swept down on the *El Gamo*.

The Spaniard's two broadsides went wide and *Speedy* ran alongside and opened fire. All the enemy had to do was to swarm over the smaller ship, but the Spanish captain had been killed and they were leaderless. *Speedy's* whole crew, except for the surgeon at the helm, clambered aboard the Spaniard and fought like tigers, while Cochrane ordered a sailor up a masthead to lower the Spanish colours. Thinking one of their officers had surrendered the ship, the Spaniards gave in, having lost more than the entire crew of the *Speedy*. Cochrane's casualties were three killed and eight wounded and many think this action the finest single-ship fight of the entire Napoleonic Wars.

Cochrane and his adoring men earned vast sums of prize money from their captures, which was fair reward as naval pay was so poor. But the Admiralty failed to buy *El Gamo*—to Cochrane's fury. He bitterly resented chair-bound Port Admirals and their henchmen who made fortunes out of prizes far in excess of the money that went to the fighting men.

Cochrane's promotion was held up because his friends upset the Admiralty by talking about him over-enthusiastically. And when even his gallant first lieutenant, Parker, was not promoted because—so said the First Sea Lord—the small number of casualties aboard *Speedy* did not warrant it, Cochrane wrote him a very rude letter. He found

One of Cochrane's most astounding feats was the capture of a Spanish frigate during the Napoleonic Wars. On another occasion (right) he turned a ship into a vast floating torpedo and destroyed a blockade of French ships.

himself ashore and Parker's career was ruined.

Now he thought he would enter Parliament and expose corruption in the Navy and in naval dockyards, from which some ships sailed so badly equipped and built that several sank with all hands. But after a short spell of peace, he was sent to the Orkneys aboard *Arab*. This ship was little better than a floating coffin.

Luckily, the Government fell and so did his enemy, the First Sea Lord, and Cochrane was given a brand new frigate, the 34-gun *Pallas*. Between January and April 1805, the frigate made £75,000 in prize money.

In 1807, he entered Parliament and launched broadside after broadside against corruption in the Navy and everywhere else he found it. The Admiralty sent him to sea to get rid of him, and he distinguished himself raiding French shipping off Spain, now a British ally, and leading landing parties against the French invaders of Spain.

In 1890 he was given the near-impossible task of burning the French fleet, then being blockaded by Lord Gambier at Rochefort. Cochrane aboard *Imperieuse* decided that fireships were not enough to destroy the French in Aix Roads and turned one ship into a vast torpedo by stacking it with gunpowder. It destroyed a boom the French had put across the harbour and the fireships sailed through.

Now was Gambier's chance to sail in and finish off the French, but he refused to budge and the chance was lost. Cochrane had to sail out. He protested strongly to Gambier, who sent him back to England. There he found himself a national hero and was knighted. But, when he heard that Gambier was to be given a vote of thanks in the Commons, he erupted even more volcanically than usual, and the Admiralty was forced to court-martial Gambier. One of the Admiral's friends was in charge and the incompetent Gambier was acquitted. Years later, Napoleon was asked for his opinion and said that Cochrane was right and Gambier was a fool. So now Cochrane was branded as the Navy's chief troublemaker, idolised by his men and his constituents and hated by Authority.

He married a young girl named Katherine Barnes, who proved a fine wife for the heroic fire-eater.

In 1814, he was jailed for fraud. There had been a plot to make money on the Stock Exchange from a rumour that Napoleon was dead. Cochrane was involved, but was probably innocent. A trial rigged by his enemies saw him imprisoned for a year and fined £1,000. He seemed finished.

He promptly escaped, then marched into Parliament and was marched out again and put in solitary confinement to the fury of his constituents. He was allowed out again after paying his fine, then re-arrested for not paying an extra £100 for having dared to escape. His constituents paid the fine, and he returned to assail the Establishment.

In 1818, his luck changed. Chile was fighting to be free of Spain and he was asked to take command of its navy. He and his wife sailed away to a continent where there were plenty of corrupt officials to remind them of home.

His exploits in South America were as fabulous as his earlier ones. He was now sailor, soldier, pirate, politician and public relations man rolled into one.

In command of the tiny Chilean Navy, he stormed fifteen strong forts at Valdiva in 1819. The next year he saved his ship almost single-handed after it had struck a rock, repairing broken pumps himself and preventing the crew from panicking. He did more than anyone to liberate Chile, then helped liberate Peru. Though wounded, he captured the Spanish flagship at Callao, watched by an audience of neutral American and British sailors.

He had to struggle to get his crews paid by the revolutionary leaders who were little better than the Spaniards they had overthrown; then, with Chile and Peru free, he helped Brazil gain her freedom from Portugal. Less successful was his attempt to help the Greeks free themselves from Turkey. Political rows, lack of men and ships, and the failure of expected steamships made him retire from the fray exhausted. He came home.

Gradually, his position improved. His enemies died and his fame was colossal. He was "pardoned" in 1832 to his extreme annoyance as he felt himself innocent, and was made a Rear Admiral; and by now he was Earl Dundonald. He tried to interest the Admiralty in steamships but failed, then in 1848, he was given command at sea again. He was 73!

In 1860, his long life ended. He was mourned by Queen Victoria and all her subjects, and by the peoples of Chile, Peru, Brazil and Greece.

With his crew close to panic after their ship had struck a rock, Cochrane himself repaired the broken pumps and restored order.

BIRDSTRIKE!

Scientists are seeking to solve a natural hazard that threatens the safety of aircraft.

IN 1960, a Lockheed Electra airliner powered by prop-jet engines was making its final landing approach to Boston airport in the United States of America. The pilot was holding the airliner steady as he saw the runway dead ahead. In less than two minutes the passengers would be feeling the slight bump as its landing wheels made contact with the ground, and their flight would be over. Then, suddenly, to his dismay the pilot saw a large flock of starlings rise into the air and fly straight across his flight-path.

It was too late for him to take any evasive action and within seconds a number of the tiny birds struck the leading edge of the aircraft's wings, and worse, a number of them were sucked into the air intakes of the engines causing one of them to fail.

Despite all he could do, the captain lost control and the plane crashed killing all those on board–

sixty-one passengers and crew.

That tragic accident, which took place more than 16 years ago, focussed attention on a flying hazard which still causes problems on airfields in different parts of the world. Although modern airliners are now constructed to withstand impacts from birds and are certainly strong enough to prevent any serious structural damage, it is trouble with the engines following a bird-strike that can be dangerous.

A bird as small as a starling entering the air intake of a large jet engine can pass through without causing serious damage–although the same cannot be said for the bird! The trouble is that a number of birds may enter the engine at the same time setting up pressures that may cause it to catch fire and disintegrate.

It is because of this possibility that airport authorities in many parts of the world, and particularly in Britain and the United States, have spent a great deal of time and money combating the problem. Many different ideas have been tried, from sound amplifiers producing noises to frighten birds away, to using birds of prey such as hawks and the peregrine falcon to discourage birds from the vicinity of airfields. At Mildenhall in Suffolk, an important United States Air Force base in Britain, two falconers are employed full-time, but they have had only limited success.

One theory about why it is that birds seem to be attracted to airfields has been put forward by scientists who have been studying their behaviour. It is thought that the vibration caused by the sound of aircraft taking off and landing causes worms to come to the surface in fields adjoining airports.

Worms are attracted to the surface by the sound of heavy rainfall (watch the birds on your lawn after a downpour!) and it may be that aircraft vibrations make a similar sound as far as worms are concerned. Naturally, the birds are quick to take advantage of any extra food supply, and flock to the area from the surrounding countryside.

Vancouver airport in Canada has a special bird problem. Large flocks of small shore birds called dunlins– and as many as 8,000 have been estimated in one flock–seem to have become accustomed to the usual deterrents such as fireworks, gas cannons, shot-guns and run-way patrol vehicles. As Vancouver is an international airport with many aircraft movements, the bird-strike danger is a constant worry to the authorities, so the problem was tackled by a special committee of the National Research Council of Canada.

Studies were carried out using live falcons and also radio-controlled model aircraft. The live falcons were seen to be effective in frightening the dunlins, but it was realised that training falcons and looking after them was both expensive and time-consuming, so the scientists came up with an idea which combines both radio-controlled models and 'falcons'.

They built a flying model of a 'falcon' which can be controlled by airport personnel, as ornithologists pointed out that birds are scared not by the sound of a bird of prey, but by its shape and outline against the sky.

Trials were carried out in 1975 when it was found that not only dunlins were scared off by the

Falcons, real and 'simulated' have proved effective in clearing birds from airfields. The radio-controlled model (top) used in Canada at Vancouver airport is powered by a small engine inside its "head" driving a propeller just above its "beak". It has wing and tail control surfaces. The graceful live falcon (left) is used at a Naval air station to keep the area clear for fast, low-flying jets.

Modern military jets are designed to "hug the ground" to escape radar detection. Flying very low and near the speed of sound, they present a great challenge to the windscreen designers. The cockpit of the big Rockwell B-1A bomber is a good example. It has one of the largest windscreens yet made and has to be able to take a birdstrike at about 660 m.p.h. and remain intact.

radio-controlled 'falcon', but also ducks, gulls and geese. Further tests are being carried out to discover if the birds are capable of learning the difference between the false falcon and a real one.

Research departments of aircraft manufacturers and government aeronautical establishments can study the effects of bird-strikes on aircraft with special equipment like that shown on this page.

A bird weighing about 4lb (1 kil. 814 grams) is loaded into the barrel of a high-powered compressed air cannon and fired at the bodywork of the aircraft under test. When the velocity of the bird striking the metal skin of the aircraft is 300mph it exerts a force of 14 tons on the part it strikes. If the speed is doubled to 600mph the effect is similar to an object hitting the aircraft with a force of 57 tons, so it doesn't require much imagination to realise the damage a large bird could do to something like a fighter plane diving low over an airfield where birds are in flight.

A Royal Air Force Canberra strike aircraft once had its thick windscreen completely shattered by a bird thought to have been an eagle, and other military planes have suffered quite severe damage to wing leading edges and air intakes.

All new aircraft types must have their windscreens tested for strength against birdstrike before they enter service. It's done by using a giant air gun (above) to hurl dummy birds at a sample windscreen with enormous force. The diagram (below) shows how the speed of an aircraft multiplies the weight of a bird on a collision course.

1·8 kilo bird at 482 km/h = 14 tons

1·8 kilo bird at 965 km/h = 57 tons

The Valley of Vision

IT was almost midnight when thunder reverberated through the Kentish hills and the summer rain came down in torrents. That summer of 1827 there had been more than one such storm and, to a certain group of young men living in the little village of Shoreham, these were nights to glory in. Many a villager on his way home late at night was startled to see these apparitions—some of whom were dressed in long, flowing robes like the Druids of old—singing eerie, ancient music and gazing intently at the sky.

This group of young men was known by the villagers as the "Astrologers", many believing the group to be practising some kind of black magic.

In reality these eccentric young men were artists and they spent the summer nights out in the open in order to study the dramatic effects of Nature—especially those effects created in the sky by the great summer tempests. These artists called themselves "The Ancients" in token of their preference for the life and customs of the past. Although on their excursions they were primarily con-

---

In a dark, lonely lane, Samuel Palmer and his friends would act out a tragedy—on the very spot where a murder had once been committed.

cerned with studying nature, their sense of the dramatic led them to sing, what was to the villagers, singularly weird music such as Locke's music for Shakespeare's "Macbeth". And, on occasions "The Ancients" would act out a tragedy in a certain dark, lonely lane which had been the scene of a murder some time before.

The leading light of "The Ancients" was a young man in his early twenties called Samuel Palmer who, at this time, was producing drawings and paintings of extraordinarily vivid power which made the usual Victorian landscape painting pale into insignificance.

Samuel Palmer was born in 1805, the son of a bookseller. He had very little formal education but a talent for drawing soon showed itself and by the age of 14 he was exhibiting at the Royal Academy and the British Institution.

Samuel Palmer was 19 when he met the man who was to influence his life and his art to an enormous extent—the poet, painter and mystic, William Blake.

Blake was ill in bed with a scalded leg when the young Palmer visited him for the first time. Palmer describes the sixty-seven-year-old Blake sitting up in a bed covered with books, hard at work and looking "like one of the Antique patriarchs, or a dying Michelangelo." The great old man was to open the young Palmer's eyes to his own imaginative powers.

NEW WORLD

It was shortly after his meeting with Blake that Palmer first came across the landscape which was to figure so prominently in his art: the countryside in and around the little Kentish village of Shoreham on the river Darent. Here, in what he called his "valley of vision", Samuel Palmer entered the rich, magical world of his imagination.

In 1827, Palmer's father retired to Shoreham, buying a fine, red-brick house, called "Waterhouse". Here were housed Samuel Palmer's circle of artist friends, "The Ancients"—Edward Calvert and George Richmond—who were frequent visitors.

The great man himself, William Blake, visited Shoreham just the once—in the year of his death, 1827,—and here at "Waterhouse" he demonstrated his clairvoyant powers in a striking manner.

It became necessary for Samuel Palmer to leave his guests, who included Edward Calvert and his wife as well as Blake, and take the coach to London. About an hour later, Blake, who was sitting at the kitchen table, put his finger to his head and said: "Palmer is coming; he is walking up the road."

The Calverts reminded Blake that Palmer had been seen off by them on the London coach. Blake simply replied: "He is coming through the wicket gate." *Moments later Samuel*

Placing his fingers on his head, William Blake told the astonished gathering that Palmer – who had left for London over an hour before—was coming back to the house.

Palmer walked in! The coach had broken down en route and Palmer had been forced to walk home.

Even after his death, the great mystic continued to influence the young Samuel Palmer, inspiring him to see in his surroundings at Shoreham a landscape that was almost supernatural.

The watercolours Palmer painted at this time, such as "Coming From Evening Church", "A Hilly Scene", "The Magic Apple Tree", are among the finest visionary landscapes ever made by an English artist. And the series of highly stylised landscapes, such as "Early Morning" and "The

Valley Thick With Corn" (which were executed in a strange, experimental technique of pen and brush in sepia mixed with gum and covered with varnish) are unique in English art.

Palmer's Shoreham pictures are full of trees heavily-laden with fruit, great cumulus clouds behind full, rounded hills and, his strongest symbol of all, the moon, which casts a warm romantic glow over his landscapes.

In a note, scribbled on the cover of a portfolio much later in life, he wrote:

"Thoughts on Rising Moon—with raving-mad splendour of orange twilight glow on landscape. I saw that at Shoreham."

Thanks to the scribes who recorded in minute detail the events of the time, we know a great deal about the people of ancient Egypt who lived in a land that has been called...

The Gift Of The Nile

WHEN the British archaeologist, Howard Carter, discovered the tomb of Tutankhamun, the one time ruler of Egypt had been dead for 3500 years. Yet so far as Carter was concerned, the young king was quite familiar. Not only his name was known, but those of his whole family, as well as the work of his father in law, Akhenaten, whose attempts at religious reform had caused so much trouble in his time. The purpose of each of the hundreds of objects discovered in the burial chamber was understood, as were the identities of the many gods whose images watched over the royal sarcophagus. In fact, although the discovery of Tutankhamun's tomb was a triumph of archaeological detection, Howard Carter already knew as much about the king as if he had been dead no more than a couple of centuries.

It is hard to believe that the storybook world of the vanished Pharaohs should be so familiar to 20th century scientists, but as long as 5000 years ago the ancient Egyptians were painstakingly writing down a history of their times. No other nation can claim a history anything like as long. And so graphic were those early scribes that today even people who usually show little interest in the past are able to produce a surprising amount of information about the great civilization that was founded beside the Nile. Almost everyone has heard of the Pyramids and the Sphinx, of Rameses, Ptolemy and Cleopatra, for there is something about the sheer magnificence of the Pharaohs that captures the imagination. After all, who can fail to be fascinated by a people who could achieve engineering feats at a time when Europe

51

was barely entering the Bronze Age?

The Greek traveller, Herodotus, wrote that "Egypt is the gift of the Nile", and certainly no other country in the world has owed its very existence to a single river. Four times the size of England, Egypt would never have been more than an extension of the Sahara desert had it not been for the river that cuts a green, fertile valley through the country from South to North. Even so, it's a narrow enough strip of usable land, nowhere wider than 24·14 km (15 miles) save for the delta region where two thirds of the population live. Ninety five per cent of the country is as parched and uninhabitable as the Sahara itself.

The centuries have changed the people remarkably little. The Egyptians of today are almost direct descendants of the men who built the pyramids, because unlike many countries, Egypt has never been occupied by great hordes of land hungry invaders. True, it has been governed by strangers, such as the Persians, Greeks, Arabs and Turks, just as from time to time influential foreign families have stayed to seek wealth and power beside the Nile. But there has never been enough good land to tempt settlers. Most of the soldiers who tramped into Egypt as part of one conquering army or another took one look at the sun blistered wastes beyond the Nile Valley and promptly decided that they were better off at home. The result is that today many a peasant farmer should be able to trace his family back for several thousand years without ever finding a relation who was anything other than Egyptian.

After enjoying almost 3000 years of stable rule under the Pharaohs, Egypt fell into a decline that was to last until the rise of British power in India gave it a new importance. In those days most people bound for India travelled by sea to Alexandria and then overland to Suez, where a ship waited to take them on through the Red Sea to the Indian Ocean. When the Suez Canal was opened in 1869 the whole world began to send its shipping through Ferdinand de Lesseps' engineering masterpiece. It was the sheer importance of this link that prompted the Egyptians to take over its control in 1956, a step that was to establish the unquestioned independence of their country for the first time in more than 2000 years.

To anyone visiting Egypt today, it seems at first to be still the same country one has read about in history books. There are the palm trees, the camels and those majestic ruins so miraculously preserved in the dry air. The desert is unchanging, and graceful feluccas still carry goods along the great highway of the Nile, making full use of the prevailing wind that enables them to sail upstream and relying on the current to carry them down.

Egypt grows cotton, maize, rice and some sugar cane, and until recently crops depended very largely on the regular summer flooding of the Nile. But the building of a great dam at Aswan has stopped this great surge of water and promises instead a controlled, all-the-year-round supply, plus the additional benefit of electric power. With land that is rich in oil and minerals, the outlook for the land of the Pharaohs is a bright one.

It was Howard Carter who uncovered the secrets of Tutankhamun's tomb (right). The Pyramids and the Sphinx (below) are among the best known monuments in the world. They are a fitting reminder of the splendours of a time when the Pharaohs ruled Egypt.

But what is it like to *be* an Egyptian? The answer depends very much on whether you happen to be a town dweller or one of the millions who work on the land. An office worker in modern Cairo usually expects to live in a flat that may not be particularly luxurious but is at least reasonably up to date. But in the villages a small farmer's home will still be made of the traditional dried mud bricks, simply furnished and packed with several generations of family.

FAMILY UNITY

This living together of children, parents, grandparents and probably a number of uncles, aunts and cousins as well is something that may seem very like overcrowding to us. But to most Egyptians it is quite natural. Almost all are Mohammedan, a faith inherited from the Arabs. Indeed, Egyptians consider themselves to *be* Arabs, and citizens of the United Arab Republic. Their religion stresses the unity of family life, and it would be unthinkable for relations to see as little of each other as is quite usual in the West. Besides, it is a fairly simple matter for the head of a household to enlarge his home if necessary, and heating is no problem in one of the hottest countries in the world!

At the end of the day a farmer will talk with his friends over a cup of coffee, taking his ease in the market place much as he has always done. It is in the cities that people are getting used to modern entertainments, such as television and the cinema.

The Aswan Dam is a symbol of modern Egypt.

Talk to a modern Egyptian, and you're likely to find that his idea of storybook Egypt differs a good deal from your own. So far as he's concerned, the treasures left by the Pharaohs are an honoured reminder of his country's past and the mainstay of a thriving tourist industry, but that is all. He is far more likely to be excited about the prospect of unlimited water from the Aswan Dam, the fact that most villages now have their own piped supply, and that 2000 much needed new doctors are graduating from medical colleges each year. Egypt, he is likely to tell you, has been famous for history long enough. Now, for the first time, its people are looking forward to an exciting future.

53

MUSIC'S MASTER JOKER

THE Parisians had become pleasure mad, those that had the money to be that is, and it infected them like a disease. On the throne sat Napoleon III, the nephew of the great Napoleon Bonaparte, and the master of the musical revels of his Second Empire was an adopted Frenchman named Offenbach, who had been born a German Jew. When the Second Empire crashed in 1870 before the sledgehammer might of Prussia, leader of the German states, Offenbach's world, as we shall see, crashed also and never completely recovered.

Jacob, later Jacques, Offenbach was born near Cologne in 1819, his father being a wandering violinist who became known as "der Offenbacher" after his native town. The children took their surname from it.

Father and son went to Paris in 1833 and the boy who was to become the master of operetta, the delightful form of light opera that he more than anyone else invented, first made his name as a serious cellist. The famous waltzes, gallops, comic songs and intoxicating can-cans came later. Not that he took life too seriously. When he was in one orchestra pit he and another cellist once took it in turns to play the notes. Meanwhile, his tunes became more and more popular, for he was soon a busy composer as well as a cellist. By the time he was 20 he was famous.

He began to dream of composing comic operas, but found that no one was interested. Even a successful little piece about a double-bass player and a cannibal queen did not lead to anything, so he finally opened a tiny theatre of his own, Les Bouffes-Parisiens. Here, and in a later theatre not much bigger, he produced operetta after operetta—some 90 in thirty years—a number of which are still famous, and whose style has influenced innumerable theatre composers since. Some of those in his debt are and were Sir Arthur Sullivan of Gilbert and Sullivan fame, Johann Strauss, the waltz king of Vienna, Franz Lehar, who wrote The Merry Widow, and the modern Americans, Cole Porter and Leonard Bernstein.

All Paris did its best to pack his little theatres, especially for his greatest successes. Best of all, perhaps, is Orphée aux Enfers (Orpheus in the Underworld), a wicked satire on the old Greek legend of the musician whose wife Eurydice dies but so charms Pluto, ruler of the infernal regions, that when Orpheus goes down to reclaim her, she is released only on condition that Orpheus does not look back at her as they leave. He cannot stand the strain and does so—and loses her.

In the operetta Eurydice is bored stiff by Orpheus's playing and eager to get down to hell to join Pluto, while Orpheus is none too keen on her. But he has to go down below to get her. After all, it is part of mythology, so he has to! In the end he is very glad to leave her there, while she is only too pleased to stay below. This is the operetta that contains the famous can-can known by millions who have never seen the work. Fortunately Sadler's Wells Opera, now the English National Opera, revived Orpheus in the 1960s and still give it, so hundreds of thousands have been able to revel anew in Offenbach's genius and high spirits.

In this operetta, and others like La Belle Hélène (Beautiful Helen) about Helen of Troy, the original audiences could enjoy characters based on well-known personalities of the day, mockery that made them scandalous. Naturally, they became more popular than ever as the word got around. We cannot follow these topical allusions today, but that hardly matters. What does matter is that the works are properly performed, for Offenbach was a master musician, much admired by "serious" composers. The Italian genius Rossini, whose own The Barber of Seville, remains one of the two or three supreme comic operas, dubbed him The Mozart of the Champs-Elysées, a marvellous tribute from a man who chose his words with care, for Mozart was considered by Rossini the greatest of all composers. (The Champs-Elysées is the famous Paris street and Offenbach's theatre was there). The great German composer Wagner admired Offenbach also, even though the latter had mocked him in one of his pieces.

The 1860s were Offenbach's greatest years, with Hélène in 1864, La Vie Parisienne (Parisian Life) in 1866 and La Perichole in 1868, based on an actual actress of that name. Also in the '60s came La Grande Duchesse de Gerolstein (1867), given in a year when a great exhibition was held in Paris. It was a satire of war and warriors and one of the characters was a "take-off" of Prussia's Iron Chancellor Bismarck, who watched a performance when visiting the capital. Around him and outside in the streets Paris was in a carnival mood, gaiety was everywhere. The Prussians seemed no threat to the mighty French Empire with its Napoleonic dreams of La Gloire, but the might of France was a sham, as Bismarck knew. He could afford to smile grimly at the mockery of himself on the stage knowing full well that one day he would bring the whole shaky edifice of the pleasure-drunk, uncaring nation tumblind down.

Meanwhile, not only Paris but all Europe was at Offenbach's feet. The works kept coming out—Bluebeard, Robinson Crusoe and dozens more. Then in 1870 France was defeated in a short campaign and the Prussians besieged Paris, from which Offenbach had wisely fled. After the war he returned to find that he was too closely identified with the old regime to be as popular as before. The Press savagely attacked him, though his music was too loved for him to be truly neglected. He turned his mind to opera. He had tried his hand at it before without real success, but now he began to dream of finishing his career with a masterpiece. He could hardly write a large-scale heroic opera, especially one based on ancient legends: he had done too much mocking in that particular line, and a sentimental love drama was not his style. Instead he chose one of the stories of the poet Hoffmann, calling his romantic extravaganza Les Contes d'Hoffmann (The Tales of Hoffmann).

This extraordinary blend of fantasy and realism has always been popular with audiences, and its Barcarolle is one of Offenbach's best-known tunes, but the composer did not live to see its triumph. It was finally produced at the Opéra-Comique theatre in Paris in February 1881 but Offenbach had died the previous October. "Make haste to stage my piece," he had implored the Director of the theatre. "I am in a hurry and have only one desire in the world—to see the premiere of my work." It was a bitter jest of the gods to forbid the master joker to see his one serious work.

The people of Paris flocked to Offenbach's theatres.

MURDER WAS THEIR BUSINESS

Burke (top) and Hare—dealers in a grim trade.

MIDNIGHT in Edinburgh and all was not well. Stealthily, men with sacks and shovels crept towards the city's burying grounds, taking no notice of the raucous shouts and songs and laughter that echoed through the narrow, foul-smelling back streets of one of the most beautiful and cultured capitals of the world.

The men, many working in pairs, knew from previous spying where they had to head, freshly dug graves that would yield up the best spoils. They went to work with their shovels, putting the earth on canvas sheets to make sure that no one knew they had been about their ghoulish business. Then, two hooks were forced under the coffin lid and tied to a rope which the night prowlers pulled until the lid gave way. Moments later the body was in a sack and the coffin lid and the earth were being put back into place. Then the journey home began, where the corpse would be put in a tea chest or some other suitable box ready for its final journey to a place where the body-snatchers knew their grisly relics would be welcome. The Resurrection Men had struck again.

This is the story, set in 1828, of the worst of them, who hit upon a plan so evil that they did not need to "work" at the trade—unless you call murder work. But first it must be explained why the Resurrection Men were needed and who availed themselves of their ghastly services.

In the early 19th century, the science of surgery was making great advances and more and more British students were learning it at home, rather than at the great European schools where many had previously gone. But one thing held them back, a serious shortage of bodies for their teachers and themselves to dissect. In fact, schools of anatomy were rationed to the occasional corpse of a criminal and that (officially) was that. So it was hardly surprising that wherever there was a school of anatomy in

Britain, the ghastly but useful trade of body-snatching flourished.

The Medical School of Edinburgh was one of the greatest of all such schools. And the most popular and renowned teacher was Doctor Robert Knox, his face scarred by smallpox which had lost him the sight of an eye. His presence, though, was as striking as his tongue was caustic and witty and his nature conceited. Over 300 students would subscribe to his courses on anatomy, and some of them acted as Resurrection Men themselves.

He alone was never short of corpses, suitably fresh, for which he paid up to £10—a considerable sum in those days. And he never asked questions about the background of the bodies that were brought to him. For him, science was the vital thing, not morality.

This made it easy for two human monsters to concoct a plan with their almost equally monstrous wives for getting rich quick. William Burke and William Hare had both come to Edinburgh from Ireland. Burke was 36, bright and strongly built, and he and his wife eked out a living buying up old boots and reselling them. Hare looked half-witted, but was more cunning and grasping even than the unspeakable Burke. Hare and his wife rented verminous beds to vagrants in their equally verminous hovel.

One November night in 1827, an old soldier died at the hovel who owed Hare £4, so he decided to sell the body. He asked Burke for his advice, and the pair decided to do business with Doctor Knox, who made them welcome at his lecture rooms and told them that he hoped to see them again.

The precious pair began to think, and decided that manufacturing corpses was better than stealing them or waiting for old lodgers to die. So manufacture them they did to the tune of at least sixteen corpses in under nine months. It was so simple they discovered. There were plenty of lonely souls in the city, people about whom

no questions would be asked. It was only too easy to spend a jolly evening with them and get them drunk, then suffocate them by hand or pillow. Burke was the killer-in-chief, being the stronger, and Hare robbed the victims after death, but both were equally guilty. So in the eyes of the public, when their story broke, was Doctor Knox, for how could such a brilliant anatomist not have recognised tell-tale signs of violence on the bodies brought to him by Burke and Hare? Even the skilful Burke was not that clever in his vile trade. Later a popular ballad was to be composed about all three of them, two lines being particularly memorable:

Burke's the butcher, Hare's the thief,
Knox the man that buys the beef.

It was an Irishwoman whose death was to bring an end to the reign of terror. She was a Mrs. Docherty, who was given a splendid party by the Burkes and Hares after Burke had turned out two of his lodgers, a

Mr. and Mrs. Gray, to house her. When she was suitably mellow, butcher Burke killed her. But the next morning when the Grays came back to have their breakfast and take away their possessions, they found that the drunken Burke was behaving very oddly. Later, with their suspicions aroused at the disappearance of the old lady, who they were told had been turned out for being impudent, they found themselves alone in the room. While collecting up their belongings and preparing to leave for good, they looked under a heap of straw which Burke had ordered them not to examine and found Mrs. Dochery. Grabbing their things, they ran out of the room, meeting Mrs. Burke, whom they questioned. She begged them not to inform and told Mr. Gray it might be worth £10 a week to him if he kept quiet, but he replied: "God forbid that I should be worth that, for I could not keep it on my conscience." Then he went to the police.

There followed arrests, the discovery of the body in Dr. Knox's cellar, and growing horror and anger in the city. But, alas, Burke had done his work well on the old lady, and the post-mortem, was inconclusive. The Lord Advocate feared that he could not get a conviction on the evidence and reluctantly decided that one of the accused must be encouraged to turn King's Evidence, which meant that he would be set free whatever his crimes. Hare was chosen, and his wife was safe because she could not be made to testify against her husband. So into the dock went Burke and his wife, who, it turned out, was not his wife. She was later released. They were tried for the killings of two other of their victims as well, but, in the event, only the murder of Mrs. Docherty mattered. Extra police were drafted in and troops stood by, so great was public fury, especially at the sight of the monstrous Hares giving evidence that would save them. Mrs. Hare had actually wanted Burke to murder Mrs. Burke sometime before, but he had refused, and was later glad that she was let off for lack of evidence against her.

There could only be one result, and 20,000 were there to watch Burke being hanged. "Burke him! Burke him!" some shouted, and a new word, "burke" or "burking", meaning smothering, entered the language. The Law could not touch the Hares, but a mob nearly caught up with Mrs. Hare before she fled to Ireland under police escort, dressed as a man; and it needed soldiers to get Hare out of Scotland and into obscurity in England. However, a story exists that workmen recognised him and threw him into a lime-kiln. He was blinded and ended his days as a London beggar. As for Dr. Knox, a committee—appointed by himself—cleared him and his reputation, but the public had other ideas and his notable career was to take a downward turn from which it never recovered. Meanwhile, the law was changed and anatomists were allowed to dissect bodies of poor people who had died in workhouses, after which they were reverently buried. Other bodies were made available and the stigma went out of dissection, so that today some folk leave their bodies to medical schools for the advancement of science and the endless fight against disease and pain.

Back to the Wild goes the 'Man of the Woods'

To save them from extinction, orang-utans are being trained to return to their natural habitat in the rain forests of Borneo.

SWINGING lithely among the saraya trees in one of the rain forests of Borneo was a hairy, long-armed and short-legged orang-utan. With her deep-set, dark eyes, she peered through the palms and bamboos that wove a network of green beneath her.

A rustling of the undergrowth far below made her clutch her baby to her chest protectively. Then, with the infant clinging to her hair and the loose skin of her chest, she was off and away, swaying and soaring from branch to vine to escape from her predator.

She was saved by her sharp ears and eyes from a predator who was not another wild animal but a man . . . a poacher whose intention had been to shoot her and capture her baby to be sold as a pet or as a zoo specimen.

This orang-utan escaped, but others have been less lucky. Poachers have captured large numbers of orang-utans. This, coupled with the fact that the forests in which they live are slowly being destroyed for agriculture, housing or timber, has reduced the population of these animals so drastically that they are now a rare and protected species.

It is estimated that there are between five and ten thousand orang-utans in the world. Each year, the total is growing smaller because their habitat is being destroyed at an ever increasing rate.

To try to reverse this trend, the World Wildlife Fund is running a scheme to train captured orang-utans so that they can be returned to the wild. These are the animals which had been taken by poachers, who had killed their parents, or were being kept as pets.

The scheme was started in 1964 after a law had come into force which forbade the killing or imprisoning of orang-utans. In the Malaysian state of Sabah, orang-utans are being freed and taught how to live in the wild again. Their progress is watched by rangers who stay in forest clearings in homes held above the swampy undergrowth on wooden uprights.

LINK WITH HUMANS

A record is kept of the way in which the released animals adapt to their life of freedom, and their behaviour is noted. For a while, the orang-utans feel a link with the men, for they have been used to the care provided by keepers.

On their walks along the jungle trails, the rangers call by name their favourites among the orang-utans. In response, the invited animal will come loping down from the branches to receive a titbit, such as a banana, from a friendly human hand.

This association with humans means a great deal to the animals, for they were used to it during their captivity. However, it is gradually broken off, and they finally become completely

In answer to a friendly call, the orang-utan swung from the tree to accept the offered tit-bit.

self-supporting in the jungle. Hopefully, these released animals will breed and so replenish the dwindling population of orang-utans.

To keep an orang-utan as a pet is a practice virtually as old as man. Archaeologists found bones in caves in West Borneo which suggested that these animals could have been kept as companions by Stone Age men.

The orang-utan is the second largest of the ape family. Its name means "man of the woods", but it is less like a man than other members of the ape tribe. Its very long arms contrast with its extremely short legs. Its head is compressed from back to front, its jaws project and its high forehead makes it look very brainy.

Home for an orang-utan and its mate is in a tree, where a nest of sticks is built. The animals retire to this at night after feeding during the day on fruit, leaves and shoots.

To get their food, they climb unhurriedly among the vines and branches, grasping these firmly with their arms and feet. Orang-utans, which have never been captured, seem to float through the trees on the swaying vines. Rarely do they miss a handhold or a foothold.

When the orang-utan picked up a piece of wood and used it as a tool it was only copying something it had seen a human do.

But an orang-utan, after being kept in a cage, seems to lose this facility for being mobile among the treetops, and some have been known to miss a branch or a vine when on the move.

Rangers who have seen this, also noted another fact which might surprise animal lovers. One day, an orang-utan was seen to pick up a branch and use it like a hammer. For a wild animal to make use of a tool is a startling occurrence. Had the animal made the discovery itself that a tool could be of use to it, a truly surprising event in animal evolution would have taken place. However, the orang-utan in this case was copying something it had seen humans do.

In these and other actions, orang-utans are very attractive creatures. Indeed, it is this aspect which encourages men to want to adopt them as pets, for they seemed like comical copies of Man himself.

Man is repaying his debt to these creatures— the debt which sadly reduced their numbers—by teaching them to live in their natural surroundings again. But when they have fully acclimatized themselves to the rain forests, Man's reward will be to see less and less of these creatures.

Orang-utans are very shy animals. When the rangers walk through the jungles in the future they will be fortunate if they so much as catch a fleeting glimpse of an orang-utan sheltering upon a high perch among the green forest canopy. When this happens, the rangers will be satisfied that they have done their job well.

Ask Me Another

1. In which European art gallery can you see Leonardo Da Vinci's "Adoration of the Magi"?
2. What is the colouring of the bird, the grey wagtail?
3. Where does the grey wagtail like to live?
4. What does the poisonous puffer fish do when taken out of water?
5. From what was Thor Heyerdahl's raft, "Kon-Tiki", made?
6. How far did Heyerdahl and his five companions sail on the raft?
7. In 1912 a man put together a collection of gyros, springs and counterweights and linked them to a biplane's controls, thus producing the first rudimentary autopilot. What was his name?
8. What are the Van Allen Belts?
9. In which ocean is the Seychelles group of islands?
10. Which is the main island of the group?
11. Which Russian Tsar ordered the building of the Trans-Siberian railway?
12. When was work started on the railway?
13. The line runs between which two places?
14. To which section of orchestral instruments do the bassoon and the Cor Anglais belong?
15. Konrad Korzeniowski wrote many novels but under a new name – what was it?
16. Which of Michelangelo's works is usually considered to be his masterpiece?
17. Who wrote an opera based on the legend of a sea captain forced to sail the stormy seas for ever in a phantom ship? What is the name of the opera?
18. What material is made by heating a mixture of sand, soda or lime, and potash to an extremely high temperature?
19. Which writer of the nineteenth century created the Frankenstein monster?
20. Who portrayed the monster in the first sound version film of "Frankenstein", made in 1931?

NOW TURN TO PAGE 127 FOR THE ANSWERS

The Patriot Who Was Beaten By An Earthquake

THE sturdy little boy with the blue eyes and curly hair gazed anxiously from the window.

"Will papa come?" he asked, for the hundredth time.

"Of course!" his nurse assured him. "You will see your papa today."

There was a commotion at the gate, and Bernardo scrambled down excitedly. His nurse held him back.

"Your papa is a very important man! You must treat him respectfully!"

Bernardo ran into the hall, keeping in the background. He had not seen his father for years. In spite of his magnificent uniform, stiff with gold braid and medals, he looked old, with a red face and greying hair. But his eyes, blue like Bernardo's, were keen, and he quickly noticed the boy.

"Well, Bernardo, and how are you?" he asked coolly. "How are you getting along with your lessons?"

"Bernardo is a good boy," said his guardian, Don Juan, quickly. "Run along, and the Governor will see you later."

The ten year old crept away in bewilderment. His own papa treating him like a stranger!

When he was older, Bernardo discovered that the Irish Governor of Chile, Ambrose O'Higgins, kept the existence of his family a great secret from his Spanish masters. Officials were not supposed to marry into local families, and he had to be very careful indeed. Without money or connections, O'Higgins had carved himself a career in the Spanish Government service.

At the time when Bernardo was born in 1778, the whole of South America was in the possession of Spain. For the past two hundred years, since the time of the Conquistadores, Spaniards had regarded the huge sub-continent as their private treasure house. It was difficult to rule, because there were four types of people there, all hating each other: the Spanish themselves, proud and haughty, who made no secret of despising those they governed; the Creoles, people of Spanish blood born in South America, many very wealthy but looked down upon; the Mestizos, people of mixed Spanish, negro and indian blood; and lastly the indians, the only real natives, who were hardly considered at all. The only way in which the Spanish could effectively rule was by repression.

Some time after the meeting with his father, Bernardo was sent to school in England. Not particularly clever, he was something rarer–kind, generous and brave. He imagined everyone to be as open and straightforward as himself but he soon discovered that this was not so. Too busy himself, Don Ambrose handed Bernardo's affairs over to people who took advantage of the boy's inexperience and his father's indifference to swindle him out of most of his allowance. During the time he spent in England, Bernardo was continually short of money.

Great new ideas were stirring at the dawn of the nineteenth century, encouraged by the success of the French and American revolutions. There were many South Americans who wished to govern themselves. Foremost was a man named Francisco Miranda, living in exile in London. Miranda taught Bernardo mathematics, and he talked to the boy about a free future for their countries. What he said appealed strongly to the young Chilean and he

Bernardo was bewildered. Why was his father treating him like a stranger?

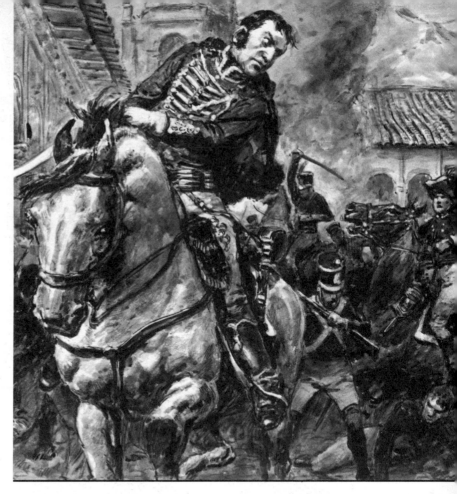

O'Higgins went to the aid of his rival, who promptly fled from the scene of the battle.

began to see the evils of Spanish rule. By the time he left London at the age of twenty-one O'Higgins was a confirmed believer in Independence.

Hardly any money had been received for Bernardo's education and it was suggested to the young man that he should go to Spain, and enlist in the army. Bernardo left his English friends reluctantly, and in Spain the army refused to accept him. He was reduced to a rather humble clerical job. He wrote to his father telling him of his poverty, but his father's silence continued, broken at last by some dreadful news. Bernardo's name had been found upon a list of Francisco Miranda's friends. This, with evidence of a conspiracy on Miranda's part, was sufficient to get O'Higgins senior, now Viceroy of Peru, dismissed from his splendid post. Overwhelmed with bitterness, he wrote disinheriting his son.

The young man felt that he must talk face to face with his father and try to explain. He scraped together the fare to Chile. But when he at last arrived, it was to find an astonishing change in his fortunes. Viceroy O'Higgins had died, and in his last moments relented and left Bernardo a large estate.

The next few years were happy ones for the young Chilean, with the pleasure of being reunited with his mother and sister, and building a comfortable home for them all. But in the world outside events were moving fast, and before long Bernardo was involved in the movement for Chilean independence. In 1808 Napoleon had deposed the Spanish king, substituted one of his own brothers, and expected the South American countries to recognise this new monarch. Naturally they refused, and saw that now if ever was the time to strike for self government.

There were still forces loyal to Spain all over South America, and the task of defeating them was very difficult, In Chile a flashy personality named Carrera was elected leader by the Freedom Fighters, and only after disastrous de-

feats did they discover their mistake. Carrera was deposed and the post of General offered to young O'Higgins, who then had to struggle against both the enemy and the supporters of the ex-commander. When it seemed as though nothing could save Chile from anarchy, Bernardo put his pride very thoroughly in his pocket and offered to serve under his rival so that their forces could be united.

Almost immediately, with typical inefficiency, Carrera was trapped in a small town called Rancagua, in the foothills of the Andes mountains. O'Higgins unhesitatingly resolved upon a rescue, although it was pointed out that Carrera would certainly not have done the same for him. "It is just because he is my greatest enemy that I must go to his help!" said Bernardo impatiently.

After bitter fighting in the little town, he was rewarded by his rival sneaking away to safety, leaving Bernardo in the midst of the action. He and his men were forced to retreat towards the mountains.

In the high passes leading to the Argentine border stood a series of travellers' rest stations. These had been built

years before by Governor O'Higgins, Bernardo's father, and now his mother and sister, with other refugees, were glad to make use of them. The ladies had had a bad time since Bernardo joined the fighting. Their estate had been over-run, their new house burnt and they themselves had been prisoners for a while. But nothing destroyed their love and faith in Bernardo.

Their courage was justified, for good news arrived. A convoy of a thousand pack mules, carrying food, clothing and medical aid, was on its way from the Argentinian General of the province, Jose San Martin.

Chile was now back in the hands of the Spanish, but on the other side of the Andes San Martin was training a mixed force of Chileans and Argentinians for the day when they might continue the struggle. Bernardo was in charge of part of the operation, having seen his mother and sister to safety. He worked frantically at raising and equipping the new army, buying great numbers of horses and mules, acquiring guns and cannon, and training men for mountain warfare. Almost

The troops hauled their artillery over seemingly impassable mountain tracks.

three years after the retreat from Rancagua, and under the direction of General San Martin, the army copied Hannibal and Napoleon, hauling their artillery across mountain tracks considered impassable. It was their plan to fall upon the enemy amidst the Chilean foothills. With Bernardo leading the first wave of troops, they met the main body of the Spanish forces at a place called Chacabuco, and the surprise of their attack completely disorganised the enemy.

A few days later, O'Higgins, San Martin and their men banqueted in the capital, Santiago.

Amidst excited scenes, Bernardo was acclaimed as Head of State, and it is not difficult to imagine how he must have felt when, largely through his efforts, Chile was proclaimed free.

The new Director soon found that nothing he had done so far was a hundredth part as difficult as the task before him. Chile was exhausted by fighting and bitterly poor, but even so the colleague who had made his victory possible, San Martin, was asking for men and materials to carry the fight into the northern kingdom of Peru.

O'Higgins realised that this could only be done from the sea—and since no Chilean navy was in being, he hired a British Admiral, Lord Cochrane, to help him found one.

Cochrane was an audacious sailor in the tradition of Drake and Nelson, and by a series of bold moves against the coastal defences of Peru he helped liberate the last stronghold of Spanish power in South America. But even whilst he was being feted in Lima, the capital, trouble was about to boil over in Chile.

Unfortunately Bernardo, like many reformers before him, tried to do too much too quickly and the things he attacked were those about which his people felt most deeply. For instance, Bernardo was shocked at the habit of burying the dead beneath the church floors, but the peasants liked to feel that their dear departed were cosily near, and did not know or care about the disease thus spread. When their Director also tried to stop popular sports like cock fighting and bull fighting, he began to appear tiresome, and —in a country where the clergy had great influence—irreligious. Whilst Bernardo struggled to get the country on its feet, opposition was growing.

Friends of his old rival Carrera were spreading dislike amongst the landowners, and from Peru and the Argentine came more requests for men and money.

Dissatisfaction came to a head with a dramatic event. Earthquakes are common on the Pacific coast of America, but one occurring just at this time convinced the Chileans that God disapproved of their Director O'Higgins. They demanded his resignation.

Astonished and resentful, it took Bernardo some time to believe that his people were in earnest, but at last with great dignity he removed his sash and sword of office and walked away a private citizen. He went to live in Peru, never to return to Chile.

Bernardo O'Higgins was not the stuff of which legends are made: with all his virtues he lacked shrewdness and ruthlessness. All the same, after his death his countrymen began to appreciate what he had tried to do for them. Now he is one of Chile's national figures: avenues, parks and statues bear his name, and a special issue of stamps was printed for the centenary of his death, in 1942, celebrating his part in the struggle for South America's liberation.

JOURNEY INTO SPACE

Space travel of the future may not be restricted to trained astronauts

MODERN transport aircraft have progressed at a fantastic rate. Fifty years ago, civil transports flew at only 160 km/h (100 mph). Today subsonic jets cruise at 960 km/h (600 mph), Concorde at 2,170 km/h (1,350 mph) and military aircraft at up to 2,880 km/h (1,800 mph) and over. This has been made possible, to a large extent, by the development of a new type of powerplant—the turbojet engine. Looking ahead to the year 2000, the jet engine may well be a thing of the past. Certainly, rocket propulsion will be used more and more during the next three decades.

A three year study was made by the British Aircraft Corporation into possible aerospace vehicles. They devised a vehicle called a multi-unit space transporter and recovery device (MUSTARD). It would consist of three modules. Each would be powered by rocket motors. The first two units would each

High speed airliner shapes of the 1970s—and a possible one which will be seen in the 1990s. Top to bottom: the Lockheed Tristar, a wide-body "airbus" which cruises at about 960 km/h (600 mph). The Bac/Aerospatiale Concorde cruising at 2,330 km/h (1,450 mph) and a possible hypersonic high-altitude giant capable of carrying 300 passengers at about 6,400 km/h (4,000 mph). Small-scale research aircraft of this shape are already being tested together with the enormously powerful engines needed to power such a craft.

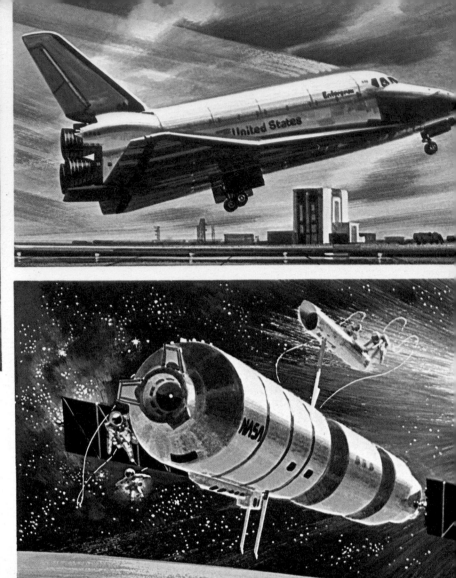

Above, the British Aircraft Corporation's "Mustard" space transporter which would have been capable of delivering payloads of 1,130 kilos (2,500 lbs) into Earth orbit. Its two outer units act as boosters and fly back to earth for reuse. The transporter also returns to Earth when its mission is complete. Above, right: the space shuttle, the first example of which is being test flown in the atmosphere—will also glide down to land as an aircraft after re-entry from space missions in orbit round the earth.

return to Earth individually after their fuel supply had become exhausted. The remaining module would continue until it reached its destination, afterwards returning to its launching site.

This project, however, has been laid to one side. Nevertheless, the Americans are pressing ahead with their space projects. When they go into space in 1979, it will be in a vehicle that is more like a space liner than the spacecraft of the past. This is called a space shuttle. It will blast off on the power of two solid-fuel rockets which at a height of 45 km (28 miles) will fall away on parachutes and drop into the sea, from where they will be recovered.

Just before the shuttle goes into orbit, its huge fuel tank will fall towards the Earth and get burnt up in the atmosphere.

But remaining in orbit will be the winged shuttle with its own smaller rockets in its tail.

Scientists will be able to work in these, for some shuttles will be big enough to house huge laboratories. The men can afterwards return to Earth in them, for the wings on the shuttle will enable it to fly back to its home base, protected by its massive heat-resisting insulation.

In fact, the space shuttle will be much more like a space airliner for the scientists, with three trained space pilots to operate it. Like any other airline crew, they will be responsible for the safety of their passengers, probably a maximum of four.

All this is not so far into the future as it seems. The first space shuttle orbiter should be glide-tested on the back of a

modified Boeing 747 shortly. If this is satisfactory, the second prototype could make the first flight into orbit in 1979.

The scientists in the shuttle will be spacemen only to the extent of becoming familiar with working and living conditions in space. Should an emergency arise, they would be conveyed by trained space men to a rescue vehicle. The craft in which they would be transported to the rescue vehicle would be shaped like a sphere, inflatable and contain everything needed to support life in the void of space.

Nothing appears to be impossible for air transport in the future. Dr. Thomas Paine, administrator of NASA—the American space organisation—has predicted that, "Through man's brains, energy and resources, life can—and life will—

NASA plans to put its first long-term space station into earth orbit in the 1980s. It would be carried up in sections, all straightforward tube shapes, by the space shuttle and linked in space to form one long unit. Here we see a shuttle unloading a fresh logistics or supply module bringing oxygen, food and other supplies. The space station's solar "wings" are spread to convert the sun's heat into electricity to power the equipment on board.

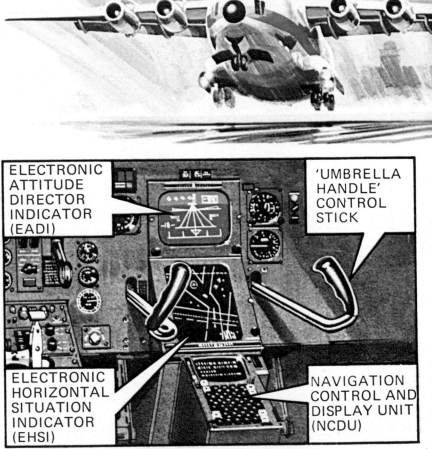

STOL performance and quiet engines using fuel sparingly will be features of most future airliners. Two examples are shown here. Top: the De Havilland Canada Dash 7, 50 passenger turboprop and (right) the McDonnell-Douglas YC15, at present a military transport.

extend itself throughout the solar system.''

Much research is being done into a hypersonic vehicle which would travel at many times the speed of sound. This could span the gap between supersonic and orbital space transport by both America and Britain. But before this step is achieved, supersonic transport will have put the whole world within a working day's travel. This may well turn out to be the fastest airborne flight that is practicable from both the operational and financial points of view. The hypersonic flights of between 6,200 km/h (3,960 mph) and 12,700 km/h (7,920 mph) may never be used for commercial passengers, as the orbital vehicle travelling at 38,100 km/h (17,500 mph) could, because of the pioneering that the Americans have already accomplished by their space flights, make any further large increase in speed of airborne flight unnecessary.

In the 1980s, the initials S.T.O.L. may be as much in everyday use as the word supersonic. S.T.O.L.–Short Take-off and Landing aircraft–might be able to solve the growing problem of congestion at major airports. S.T.O.L. airliners could be operated from small airfields, from the top of a multi-storey building, or platforms built over motorways. This type of aircraft could be in service within five to ten years if the noise problem can be overcome. A V.T.O.L.– Vertical Take-off and Landing– airliner will eventually be operating, but it will take many more years to develop, and is

ELECTRONIC ATTITUDE DIRECTOR INDICATOR (EADI)

'UMBRELLA HANDLE' CONTROL STICK

ELECTRONIC HORIZONTAL SITUATION INDICATOR (EHSI)

NAVIGATION CONTROL AND DISPLAY UNIT (NCDU)

An airliner cockpit for the future which is being developed in America. The "umbrella handle" controls leave the pilot a clear view of his electronic aids–the EADI shows all the information to fly the aircraft safely, the EHSI shows its position in the airways on a "moving map" and the NCDU and its computers can be instructed by push-buttons on the panel to navigate and pilot the entire flight and then land the aircraft automatically using other electronic equipment on the ground.

unlikely to be operating before the early 1980s.

The commercial pilot's job is becoming more technically complicated. When he is working towards his commercial pilot's licence he moves into a realm where he could fly by push buttons if necessary. He must, therefore, have a complete understanding of how these push buttons work, rather than just sitting at the controls. Obviously he has always got to be able to take over instead of allowing all the advanced gadgetry virtually to run the plane for him.

Secret in a Sunbeam

The mouse in the jar was drowsy from the lack of oxygen until Joseph Priestley placed the jar in the sunlight. Strangely, inexplicably, the mouse revived.

JOSEPH PRIESTLEY lowered a lively, wriggling mouse into a glass jar. He dropped a few sprigs of mint beside the mouse and then put the lid on the jar.

It was 1771 and Priestley, a Yorkshire clergyman and self-taught scientist, was about to open up a path of scientific exploration that was, eventually, to reveal one of the secrets of life.

Because the jar was airtight, the oxygen in it was eventually very nearly all used up by the mouse. This was apparent because the animal became sleepy and slow in its movements.

Priestley then carried the jar from the gloomy room to the window ledge. He thrust back the curtains so that the strong sunlight shone upon the jar.

As the warm rays played upon the jar's contents, the mouse gradually began to revive. The only possible explanation was that it was, somehow, getting oxygen to breathe? But how –in an airtight jar?

At that time, oxygen was an unknown gas, for it was not discovered by Priestley until three years later. But his experiments had shown him that plants had a part to play in the creation of the air we breathe.

And this experiment with the mouse had proved it. The sunlight, shining upon the mint in Priestley's jar, had liberated air which the mouse was able to breathe and so survive.

But how was this made possible? Priestley must have pondered upon this problem as he replaced the now fully-revived mouse in its cage and began to write notes on his experiment.

It was an enigma which was to remain unsolved until modern times when scientists finally unlocked the door on one of life's mysteries.

One of the substances making up a plant is called chlorophyll. This is a material which gives a plant its green colour. The action of light on chlorophyll brings about a chemical change. This produces the sugar, starches, fats and protein which keep a plant alive. At the same time, it makes oxygen. And this process, which has been going on for many millions of years, has made the Earth's atmosphere on which we depend.

The scientists have coined a name for this process. They call it photosynthesis, a term which means "made by light".

And it is an apt description of the process which starts with the sunshine reaching the plant. When the rays penetrate the outer covering of a leaf they reach the chloroplasts, which are microscopic specks inside each of the leaf's cells.

Radiation from the sun is captured by the chlorophyll and puts the chloroplasts to work in the manufacture of sugar. The plant needs some of this sugar to make new growth. Other sugar goes into the plant's fruit or seeds or, in the case of a tree, makes new wood.

Photosynthesis feeds the world, because the sun's radiation is captured by the plants which either we or animals eat. We then feed on the animal's products, such as milk, or eat its meat.

Photosynthesis is something that only the plants can do. Our benefit comes when we eat the plants or devour other animals that have fed on the plants. Therefore, photosynthesis feeds the world.

But it does more than that. To make its sugar, a chloroplast uses air and water, carbon and hydrogen, and oxygen–and in the process it makes a lot of oxygen which it does not need. This oxygen flows into the atmosphere and becomes part of the air we breathe.

The process, which makes food for the plant and enough oxygen to spare some for us as well, takes place in the leaf, which draws moisture from the stalk and carbon dioxide from the air. Minerals from the soil flow to the leaf through the stalk in the form of sap. When the sun shines upon it, photosynthesis works its wonder, and out flows oxygen to replenish the air. And food for the plant is made at the same time.

All plants are able to function in this way, but the best synthesizers are the grasses, which consist almost entirely of leaf, and so present a large area to the sun. Because of their slender shape, they grow very close together and so, for the area of earth they occupy, do better than any other plant in the creation of oxygen. Included in the grass family are wheat, barley, oats, maize, sugar cane and rice, which make up the staple food of Man. These are prime examples of photosynthesis at its most efficient.

And as plants give us a helping hand by topping up our oxygen supply, so do the plants which flourish beneath the sea do a similar job for the fishes. About 70 per cent of the Earth's surface is covered by sea. Sunlight pours through this to the plants which are carrying on the job of photosynthesis which they began when the Earth was surrounded by poisonous gases thousands of millions of years ago.

The seas' busiest plants in this respect are the algae. These range from single-celled plants to large, strap-shaped seaweeds many metres long. It is the green species which contain chlorophyll and photosynthesize like the land plants.

Most of the undersea photosynthesis is carried on by minute algae known as diatoms. These are single-celled plants which may be either joined to other plants or be free-swimming. Usually they multiply by splitting in two.

Diatoms provide food for zooplankton, such as jellyfish, arrow worms and many tiny sea animals which all live permanently in the floating state. In turn, these are eaten by herring, some sharks and even whales. And so the energy made by the sunshine and minerals from the sea bed is carried on through the creatures who eat the plants which make it, and the animals which devour the creatures, ultimately to man who eats the fish from the sea.

All this has been known since the beginning of the century, but how it works was not known

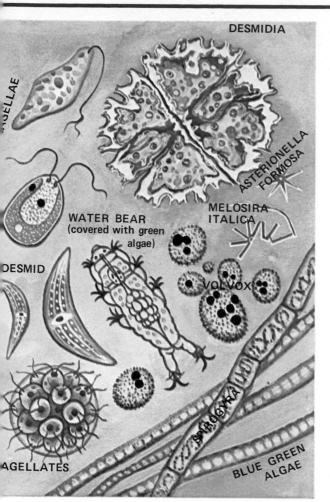

Most of the undersea photosynthesis is carried on by minute algae known as diatoms. These are single-celled plants which usually multiply by splitting in two.

DESMIDIA

FLAGELLAE

ASTERIONELLA FORMOSA

MELOSIRA ITALICA

WATER BEAR
(covered with green algae)

DESMID

VOLVOX

SPIROGYRA

BLUE GREEN ALGAE

FLAGELLATES

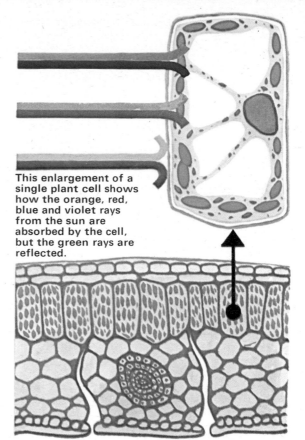

This enlargement of a single plant cell shows how the orange, red, blue and violet rays from the sun are absorbed by the cell, but the green rays are reflected.

Oxygen is released from the water in green plant cells by photosynthesis. This is shown in the diagram below in which bacteria which need oxygen gather near a strip of green alga lit by a point of light.

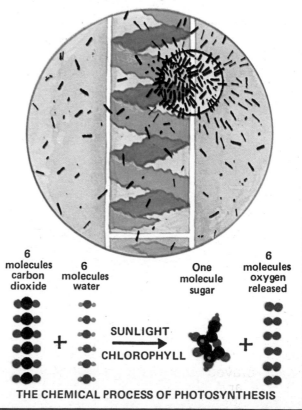

until less than thirty years ago. Then it was learnt that when radiation from the sun reaches a plant, the molecules of chlorophyll accept the orange-red and the blue-violet rays, but reflect the green rays. Leaves look green to us because we can only see the rays they reflect and not those which they absorb.

The light rays set the chlorophyll molecules buzzing with activity. From the water contained in the leaf, they snatch a hydrogen atom or an electron. Or they may pass on an electron to an atom which is reluctant to receive it. The result is like a busy city centre. But instead of cars coming and going, sometimes colliding, molecules are shooting here and there, crashing into each other, splitting, joining up, snatching up electrons or casting them off.

During all this frantic hustle and bustle, oxygen flows off, a valuable by-product of the main purpose of this activity, which is the creation of sugar from the joining together of the atoms of carbon, hydrogen and oxygen.

If sunbeams contain the secret of life, the worker of the miracle that converts this secret into food for all living things is chlorophyll, the wonder-worker of the universe.

6 molecules carbon dioxide + 6 molecules water → SUNLIGHT CHLOROPHYLL → One molecule sugar + 6 molecules oxygen released

THE CHEMICAL PROCESS OF PHOTOSYNTHESIS

THEY WENT TO AFRICA

The Dark Continent—that was the name that Africa once bore. Europeans had gained footholds at many points in the coastal areas, but it was not till the close of the 18th century that intrepid explorers began to probe the secrets of its mysterious interior. Thereafter a succession of travellers braved the many dangers—from disease and climate, fierce animals and hostile inhabitants. Some, like the coura-geous Mary Kingsley, went in pursuit of knowledge in their chosen subjects; some, like the great David Livingstone, were standard-bearers for civilisation; others, such as Speke and Baker, went to Africa to safisfy their love of adventure and sense of achievement.

In the following pages we look briefly at the exploits and journeys of just six of these explorers . . .

Samuel Baker 1821-93

AS leader of an expedition sponsored by the Royal Geographical Society, Samuel Baker set off up the White Nile in 1861, in search of the river's source. He also had the task of locating John Speke, who was seeking the source from another direction. Baker, with his intrepid and beautiful Hungarian-born wife, Florence, found Speke at Gondokoro. The Bakers then pushed on, suffering great hardships. Their boat had to be hauled by tribesmen. Eventually they discovered a great lake, which they named Lake Albert, after Queen Victoria's husband.

John Hanning Speke 1827-64

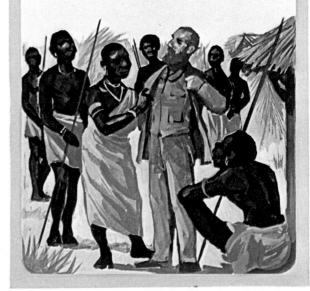

IT was with the equally famous Richard Burton that Speke set off across East Africa to find the true source of the Nile. When Burton was struck down by illness, Speke went on alone. He encountered a tribe ruled by the aged Queen Ungagu, who subjected his clothes and his person to a close inspection, and was reluctant to let him go. Managing to get away, Speke came at last to the shores of Lake Victoria, and rightly concluded that its waters fed the Nile. On a later expedition he located the outlet from the lake and went on to meet Baker.

Mungo Park 1771-1806

A YOUNG Scottish doctor, Mungo Park was the first European to shed some light on the course and origin of the River Niger. In 1895 he started out up the Gambia. He had to contend not only with the difficulties of the country, but also with the hostility of Arab slave-traders, who took him prisoner. He escaped with only his horse and his compass. At last, in July, 1896, he reached Segou. There, as his journal records, he saw "the majestic Niger flowing slowly eastward." On a later expedition he lost his life during an attack by natives.

Alexander Laing 1793-1826

A LEXANDER GORDON LAING made no great discoveries, but is famous as the first European to make the hazardous journey to Tombouctu –and for his tragic end. His journey took over a year to complete. He suffered terrible privations, and once received severe wounds at the hands of Touaregs who treacherously attacked him. On August 13th, 1826, he entered the ancient city, where he was received with suspicion. Eventually he left Tombouctu, under the "protection" of Sheik La-beida. But two days later the sheik had him killed.

David Livingstone 1813-73

UNSURPASSED among African explorers was the missionary Dr. Livingstone. As well as discovering the Victoria Falls and Lake Nyasa, he crossed the continent from coast to coast. His aim was to open Africa to civilisation, and free its peoples from the slave trade. When no news of Livingstone had been received for some years, journalist Henry Stanley was sent to find him. After their historic meeting in 1871, Livingstone attempted one more expedition. Now ill and weak, he was borne in a litter, and death overtook him before he could complete it.

Mary Kingsley 1862-1900

ONE of the most remarkable figures in the history of African travel was a woman—Mary, niece of the author Charles Kingsley. She made two extended journeys in West Africa, studying native religions and collecting specimens of insect and other life. In the course of her travels she explored much of the West Coast from Freetown to Luanda. She was a brilliant writer, describing such experiences as falling into rivers and game-pits, and the occasion when she was reduced to trading articles of clothing to obtain supplies and assistance from the natives.

The Sundew.

Sarracenia - or pitcher plant.

The Bladderwort.

INSECTS BEWARE

Not all plants are as harmless as they look . . . .

MOST green plants obtain all their food from the air and from the soil. They are independent of other organisms for their nourishment. There are a few, however, which lack the essential nutrients in their surroundings and thus are compelled to obtain food some other way. A very few plants growing in boggy and acid soils (which are low in nitrogen, an essential nutrient) out of necessity have found a way of supplementing their food supply by capturing and digesting small animals and insects. These are the carnivorous plants.

Growing in the bogs among the bog moss can be found a low-growing plant with simple white flowers on leafless, slender stems. It is called the Sundew and insects beware for it will entice and entrap you!

The leaves of the Sundew are arranged in a rosette on long stalks clothed with fine hair. Each of these glandular hairs secretes a clear, sticky fluid which glistens like a dew-drop in the sun and has a fragrance similar to honey. These sweet-scented, glistening glands, together with a red colour dissolved in the sap which suffuses the green leaf, attracts insects and small animals. Once these touch the glands they will be captured by the fluid. As they attempt to escape they become even more firmly held as through their struggle they stimulate nearby hairs which quickly bend towards the insect. The prey becomes finally enmeshed in the bent, glandular hairs and dies in this temporary stomach.

Digestive juices are then excreted by the glands and these break down the softer portions of the victim's body, just as food in our stomachs is digested by gastric juices. Later the digested matter is absorbed, again through the glands.

There are, of course, many plants which have sticky stems, flowers or leaves which trap small animals, particularly insects, but there are very few which actually digest and absorb their remains. It is these latter plants which are called carnivorous or, sometimes, insectivorous. There are about 450 species, of which some are fungi but the majority are flowering plants.

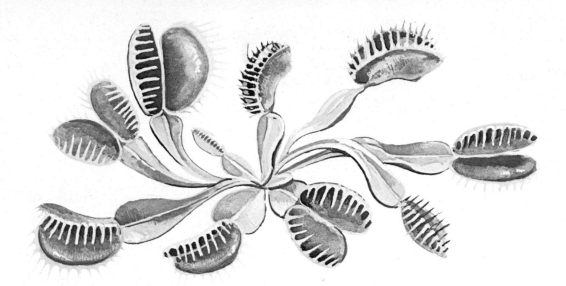

The mechanism found in these plants for trapping and digesting can vary considerably, from the active type such as the Sundew to the passive type, where no movement of any part of the plant is involved.

The pitcher plants are the best examples of the passive types where the prey simply falls into a trap. The leaves of the pitcher plant, *Sarracenia*, are exceedingly long, the sides curling together to form a tube. The top of the tube is smooth and slippery and any insect crawling along the top has to be very careful if it is not to slide down the tube which forms an erect and static trap! Once the insect falls inside, it is submerged in a fluid where it drowns and rots. The decomposed prey will later be absorbed by the plant.

DEADLY TRAP

One of the most interesting active mechanisms is to be found in the carnivorous plant with the most deadly and exotic of names, the Venus Fly Trap. The leaves of this fatal plant are hinged and have long, stout, upcurving teeth. Should a fly or other insect alight, the two halves of the leaf fold upwards like a hinge. When this happens the teeth meet and interlock so that the insect is imprisoned. The fluid secreted from the glandular hairs inside the leaf completes the digestion of the victim.

Another plant with an active mechanism is the Bladderwort which lives submerged in deep pools and canals and bears small bladder-like structures on its leaves. Each bladder has a narrow mouth supplied with a trap door. The bladder acts as a trap by sucking in any nearby small water animal or algae. Once the bladder is full the trap door closes. Digestive juices dissolve the body of the prey and this enriched fluid is absorbed by the glandular hairs. When the bladder is empty the trap door will be all set for the next visitor!

The Venus Fly Trap (above) grips its victims between the strong up-curving teeth of its leaves. The pitcher plant (below) relies on its slippery top to surprise its victims. The insects simply slide to their doom.

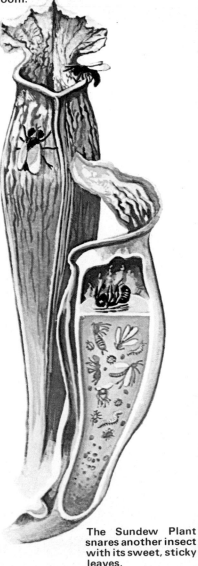

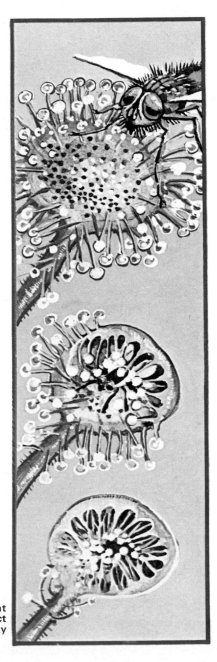

The Sundew Plant snares another insect with its sweet, sticky leaves.

BETTER SAFE THAN SORRY

Every year in Britain more than 6,000 people are killed, and about 80,000 seriously injured on our roads as a result of accidents caused by vehicles of one kind or another.

In order to realise how dreadful this loss of human life is, imagine a town the size of Slough in Buckinghamshire, or perhaps Woking in Surrey, and then think of every inhabitant being either killed or badly hurt so that the town is practically wiped out!

Government statistics show that the people who suffer most in road accidents are pedestrians, followed by motor-cyclists and the drivers and passengers in motor cars. Great efforts have been made to help pedestrians avoid accidents by providing Zebra Crossings, "walk-overs", underpasses, railings at road junctions, warning notices etc., but in the end it is the pedestrians themselves who must take care when they are crossing roads or walking in areas where traffic is moving.

Motor cyclists suffer in accidents, not necessarily because they don't take care or are bad drivers, but because they are very vulnerable to damage to themselves when they fall off their machines which is why the Government made the wearing of crash helmets compulsory. It might be a good idea if pedal cyclists wore them too.

The vehicles which can provide the best safety measures on the road in case of an accident is the ordinary family motor car. Big improvements have been made by manufacturers around the world, and research into ways of making cars even safer never stops.

One of the companies which devotes a great deal of time and money into road vehicle safety is the *Volkswagen* car company of Germany. At their huge Research and Development Centre in Wolfsburg, engineers specialising in vehicle safety continually carry out experiments to find ways of making cars safer.

Vehicle safety is divided into two main areas: *active safety* which consists of measures designed to prevent accidents happening at all, and *passive safety*, which is aimed at reducing the effects and consequences of accident damage.

To help them with their research work *Volkswagen* have installed a machine called a 'driving simulator' which is connected to a computer. The simulator is very similar to those used to train airline pilots. In the simulator a driver's reactions can be studied and measured, without endangering his life, by trying to reproduce an actual "accident".

The simulator can "rebuild" an existing car design in a matter of seconds, for example from front wheel drive to rear wheel drive, and can then check the effects on the way the car handles. Engineers can also reconstruct the same road conditions they have previously used in an experiment so that they are able to compare the

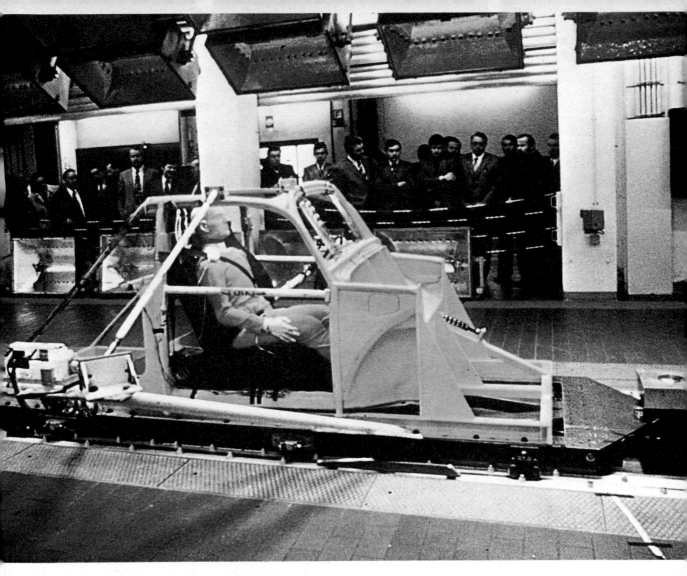

effects of design changes with great accuracy.

Other things which the "computer car" can do is investigate the medical aspects of road safety. For instance, how does a driver's behaviour change when he is tired? How does he react to certain dangerous situations which can occur on the road? How do certain combinations of alcohol and medicines affect driving ability? Above all, of course, an "accident" at the wheel of the simulator does no harm to the driver, except possibly to make him feel rather foolish when he makes a mistake that could have cost him his life had he been driving a real car on the road.

One thing this simulator cannot do is measure the effects of a crash on the human body. The experts need to know just how much the human body can stand—the maximum impact which the head with its vital control centre, the brain, or the rib cage, trunk, knee or thigh bones can withstand.

Obviously it is not possible to use real people in 'crash' studies so at the Research Centre their place is taken by a whole family of dummies, who willingly risk their necks in crash testing. The dummies' bodies are equipped with elaborate instruments which can record what happens to the various parts when they are thrown about inside a car as it crashes.

The 'family' is a large one consisting of 50 men, two women and three children. The head of the

In the pictures above and left a sled-like instrument is being used to test the effect of restraining systems during collisions. Below: the purpose of this experiment is to study the result of impact against a steering wheel.

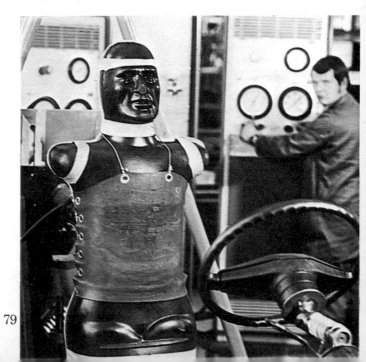

family is a dummy named *Oscar Humanus*. He is the most humanoid of what could be a group of robots out of a science fiction film. Oscar has been made so that each section of his body is matched as closely as possible to that of a human body. His ceramic leg bones (fortunately replaceable) will fracture under a severe blow. In addition he is capable of exhibiting and recording injuries to soft areas of the body.

Oscar is expensive–he cost 60,000 German Marks, or about £13,500, and like his relatives he is constantly being re-equipped to the latest technical standards. Volkswagen feel their dummies should be well treated because after all, they risk their lives for our benefit!

Since it is almost impossible to reconstruct an accident from statements made by witnesses and the people involved, the test dummies fill the gap. They are run over under typical conditions, and high-speed cameras record every detail of the movements they make. Readings transmitted by radio or wire from instruments inside the dummies tell the engineers what injuries they would have suffered.

Another safety device being tested by car manufacturers is the "air-bag" which inflates instantly when a car suffers an impact, and comes between the occupants and the car interior to save them from serious injury. Although these air-bags are effective, they have drawbacks. They will normally only be brought into action and inflated at an impact speed of more than about 24 km/h (15mph), while car safety-belts protect the occupants even during quite minor impacts, or sudden emergency stops.

In addition to this, even if a possible accident situation develops at high speed, the driver quite often manages to apply sufficient brake to reduce speed considerably before the crash occurs. Unfortunately, the propellant devices used to inflate the air-bags are then released with the same violence as in a severe pile-up. The bags are actually inflated in a fraction of a second–an experience of noise and sudden pressure which most people would not like to have. In spite of these difficulties, experiments with this type of safety device are continuing.

Seat belts are still the most widespread safety measure in cars, and car makers together with the firms who make the belts themselves, are trying all the time to improve them.

The belts must, at present, be fastened by hand and although fastening them is comparatively easy, the loss of comfort and freedom of movement when the belts are in position often discourage people from using them. Automatic inertia-reel belts which allow the wearers to lean forward and perform various other movements without restriction, are an important advance. These can also be operated with one hand and therefore put on while the car is in motion.

In spite of this, however, efforts are now being made to design a new 'passive belt system' where an automatic mechanism makes sure that the belt moves into position as soon as the driver or passenger enters the car and closes the door.

One experimental *Volkswagen* car, built to United States vehicle safety requirements, has seat belts which tighten pneumatically when the doors are closed. They are provided for both front and rear passengers, and propellant capsules tauten the belts even more to hold the wearers against their seats when a violent impact occurs.

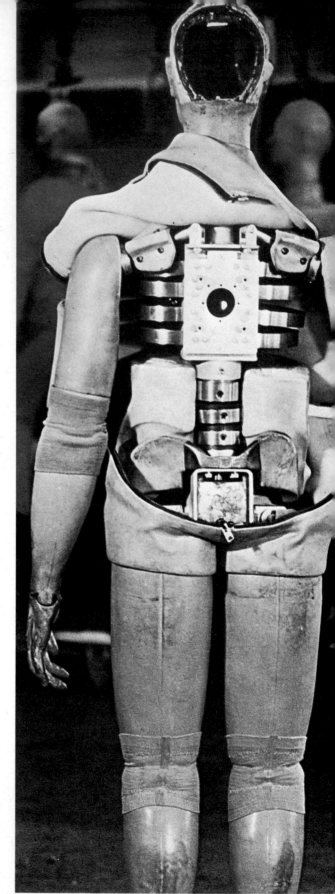

Packed inside the test dummies are instruments which record the effects of mocked-up accidents. The equipment is thoroughly checked and maintained to ensure a high standard of accuracy.

EVERYONE knows about Sinai. It's a battlefield. In history books it's fought over by ancient Egyptians, Israelites, Persians, Greeks, Romans, Saracens and Crusaders. More recently the British and the Turks had their dust-up in Sinai. In modern times it's been an arena for Arabs and Israelis.

Lots of people seem to think it's one of those ideal places for man's least pleasant pastime–war–being all desert, sand and rock with no civilians to get in the way. This is far from true. Certainly most of Sinai is a bleak and inhospitable place, but it's much more than just a battlefield. Sinai has people and an incredible history, plus animals, birds and plants in surprising variety. It also has great mineral wealth and future agricultural possibilities.

Though it looks like a great triangle stuck between Africa and Asia, the peninsular of Sinai is a pretty varied sort of place. To the north there's the Mediterranean Sea with its straight coastline broken only by Lake Bardawil. This region is relatively low lying with gentle hills and enormous sand-dunes up to 30 metres high.

Further south there is a gaunt limestone plateau which has been the real "battlefield" in most of Sinai's modern wars. It also is crossed by two vital roads. One starts from Ismailia, over the Suez Canal and goes towards Beersheba and Hebron. Finally there is the southern road called Darbel Hajj, or the "Pilgrim's Road". This leaves the Suez Canal, climbs through the Mitla Pass and so down across Sinai towards Aqaba in Jordan. From there it turns southwards to Mecca and Medina, the Holy Cities of Saudi Arabia.

Between the Gulfs of Suez and Aqaba, where Sinai tapers to a point at Ras Muhammad in the Red Sea, the geography is entirely different. This is a spectacular land of deep "wadis", or seasonal river courses, jagged desert mountains and the soaring peaks of Jebel (Mount) Catherine, Jebel Musa and Jebel Serbal. It is also a land of dazzling beaches and ink-blue seas.

Most of Sinai is barren, despite the labours of ancient and modern man. Not all of it, however; nor is this harsh land too tough for Nature and the life she brings to such unexpected places. Although Sinai has no permanent rivers, winter storms, heavy dew and the melting mountain snows of Spring provide water for the peninsula's many oases. Vegetation is sparse but it is there none the less –trees like acacia, tamarisk, caper bushes, broom, juniper, mangrove and of course palms.

There are animals as well, shy and camouflaged to merge with their savage surrounding. Apart from semi-wild camels and donkeys, mice, dormice, hedgehogs, hares, sand foxes, goats, ibex, gazelles, bats, sand plovers, the Desert Horned lark, the Trumpeter Bullfinch, the rare Hume's Tawny owl, quails, ravens, partridges, warblers and the little Sinai Rose finch, all make their homes in Sinai.

Reptiles are also common, as is only to be expected in such hot, dry, desert surroundings. They include the Sinai "hardoun" otherwise called the bright-eyed agama, the monitor lizards and the horned viper which has an even more colourful name in Arabic–Abu Genabia or the "Father of Going Sideways"

Off the coasts are fish and corals in unlimited variety.

Very few places can have had a longer written history than Sinai. It first seems to have been referred to in that mysterious year the archaeologists call "X+2", during the reign of Pharoah Udimu. This was shortly after Egypt was unified by the First Dynasty almost three and a half thousand years B.C.!

The reasons why it was mentioned are strangely similar to the reasons why Sinai and the Middle East as a whole generally get into modern newspapers–trade, mineral wealth and defence. In those days the mineral wealth in question was copper and malachite rather than oil. The former was used in weapons and tools, the latter for medicine and for eyeshadow. Later on Sinai's wealth of precious turquoise encouraged mining expeditions to fight their way into and out of Sinai against local bedouin tribes.

THE PERFECT PLACE TO FIGHT A BATTLE

One scene carved on rocks near Sinai's mines shows King Semerkhet, also of the First Dynasty, battling with a local chieftain.

When ancient Egypt was strong she ruled most of Sinai, but in Egypt's bad times the peninsula reverted to the local tribes. The mines were still vital, however, and that great warrior Pharaohs Tuthmosis III, called himself the "beloved of Hathor, Lady of the Turquoise". This is recorded on yet another rock-carving near the Sinai mines in an area not surprisingly called Wadi el Mukatab, the Valley of Inscriptions.

Sinai's ancient wealth looks as if it died out or was forgotten in later ages. The Assyrian and Babylonian Empires didn't bother with it much, and by that time the Egyptians were not in a fit state to control all the peninsula themselves. The Persians apparently ignored it, as did Alexander the Great who left it to the local Arab tribes. Even the Romans didn't get around to annexing Sinai until 105 A.D., adding it to the province of Arabia-Petraea.

That was just about the state of affairs when the Arab World, and much else besides, was welded into the enormous Empire of the Muslim Khalifs in the 7th century A.D. Since then Sinai has been solidly Muslim and Arab, although various local or alien conquerors have now and then tramped across its unwelcoming surface. Each set of rulers seem to have left their own dusty ruins in Sinai. At Qalah Jindi, just south of the notorious Mitla Pass, there is an early Saracen fortress, and on a rocky islet only a few hundred metres from the Sinai shore in the Gulf of Aqaba stands a beautiful Crusader castle once called the Isle de Graye.

Meanwhile the people of Sinai, most of whom are the nomadic bedouin, have lived out their hard and poverty stricken lives. Not surprisingly they grabbed whatever chances they could to make life a little easier. Sometimes they robbed travellers and pilgrims or, in more recent ages, smuggled drugs from the east into Egypt. This was a dangerous game, but one which the sharp-shooting bedouin played quite successfully against the hopelessly outnumbered Egyptian Frontier Forces. Only with the creation of the Egyptian Air Force in the 1930s, using De Havilland Moths, Avro biplanes and three-engined Fokker-Avros, could these illusive Sinai smugglers be tracked down and Egypt's drug problem brought under control.

After the Second World War things started to look up a bit for the people of Egypt's neglected Sinai province. Manganese, oil, phosphates, lead, zinc, copper, bitumen, malachite, iron, coal and turquoise were discovered, or rediscovered, in Sinai. In 1960, after repairing the havoc caused by retreating Israelis following the Suez War, Egypt mined almost 300,000 tons of valuable manganese. More recently tungsten and feldspar have been discovered; perhaps also bauxite from which aluminium is made. In fact Sinai has proved to be a real "Aladdin's Cave", a treasure store of minerals needed by modern industry.

Some development has already taken place, both by Egypt and by the occupying Israeli military authorities. Oilfields and their installations around Abu Rudays and Belayim on the Gulf of Suez have been a savage bone of contention in the Arab-Israeli conflict, frequently being damaged by the aircraft and commandos of both sides.

In fact Egypt only got these Sinai oilfields going seriously in 1957, but by 1966 they already accounted for two-thirds of the country's total output.

If oil is "black gold", then water is "white gold" in the dried up world of the Middle East. Before large-scale irrigation schemes began, cultivation was limited to a few areas in Sinai. Apart from the

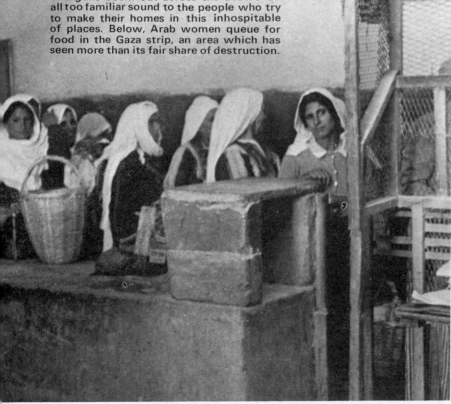

The guns boom out across the desert—an all too familiar sound to the people who try to make their homes in this inhospitable of places. Below, Arab women queue for food in the Gaza strip, an area which has seen more than its fair share of destruction.

famous St. Catherine's monastery, which was probably founded in 527 A.D. and is inhabited by Egyptian monks of the Greek Orthodox Church, most settlements were either along the main roads or on the coast.

At the north-eastern corner of Sinai stands the little town of El Arish, the original administrative capital of the peninsula prior to the 1967 Arab-Israeli War. It was a busy and prosperous area and Egyptian land reclamation programmes had pushed back the desert all around. El Arish itself was a market town with splendid groves of palm trees that produced some of the finest dates in the whole Middle East. It also had superb beaches and was a holiday resort for people from both Egypt and the Gaza Strip. In 1967, however, a quarter of the area's population fled from the invader, westward across the Suez Canal.

Nearby almost two hundred bedouin families had been settled in the new Nasser Village. Each had up to five acres of land, plus free medical services and seeds to get their farms going. Apart from a cattle breeding project and an experimental chicken farm, important new crops were introduced such as the valuable castor oil plantations.

Now that Egypt has regained control of these lands immediately east of the Canal, perhaps work can start again on a huge and ambitious irrigation scheme that was started before the June War of 1967. Maybe this could be a turning point in the struggle to change Sinai from a blood-soaked battlefield into a land of peace and fertility.

Will these young people who live in the Gaza Strip be allowed to grow up in peace ?

MYSTERY BEHIND THE MASTERPIECE

Why would the metal in the furnace not melt? It was a question that was not to be answered until centuries later.

DESPITE the intense heat, the metal refused to melt. The copper and tin that should have been fused into bronze, remained stubbornly solid.

To the workmen toiling beside the glowing furnace in Benvenuto Cellini's little workshop in 16th century Florence, the metal's reluctance to liquefy was a mystery.

In an effort to raise the temperature of their furnace, they piled more and more pine logs on to the fire. And they blocked off an open side of the workshop with an old carpet to keep out the wind. One result was that the roof caught fire, although it was put out by a fortuitous rainstorm.

But the metal? No amount of heat would make it melt. In despair, one of the workmen went to Cellini, who was lying in bed feverishly ill in the house next door. Ranting at the men's "incompetence", Cellini rushed from his bed to the foundry, and found the men about to go on strike because they did not want to be associated with a failure. Snorting, Cellini began flinging pewter plates and pots –and an overlooked ingot of tin –into the mixture.

Slowly, the copper began to respond to the injection of tin –for pewter is mostly tin, and tin is what bronze needs to become fluid at the temperature attainable in a wood-fired furnace. But why had not the bronze melted in the first place? This was a question that was to

remain unanswered for centuries, when the reason for the difficult birth of Cellini's work of art was at last discovered.

It had all begun because Cellini, a genius of a goldsmith, wanted to make something by which he would always be remembered. Most of the wonderful things he made in gold have been melted down and their jewels removed. The only piece remaining that can be attributed to him with absolute certainty is a salt cellar in the Imperial Treasury at Vienna. This was made for Francis I of France.

To gain immortal fame, Cellini knew that he had to make a piece of sculpture that would last virtually for ever. Fortunately, he found a patron who was willing to share in this fame and pay all the bills. This was the wealthy Duke Cosimo I de Medici, who readily commissioned Cellini to make him a statue.

The subject they chose was Perseus, the Greek god, who was to be shown with his foot resting upon the slain body of the Medusa, a mythological creature with snakes for hair and the ability to turn anybody who looked at her into stone. Perseus had overcome this difficulty by slaying the Medusa while watching her reflection in his shield.

Such a statue would flatter Duke Cosimo's ego and give Cellini just the subject he wanted for his masterpiece. After a while, Cellini showed

the Duke a clay model of the statue which he had in mind. Cosimo was delighted and despatched Cellini with orders to start work at once on the full-sized statue. But Cosimo had to be patient, for Cellini's life was a stormy one. He was often put into prison for his escapades, and frequently he had to flee for his life. But because his work was in such great demand, he was often pardoned and brought back to renew his labours.

Three years after Cosimo had approved the model, all that Cellini had to show was the statue's base and the headless Medusa, all cast in bronze. Cosimo had supplied Cellini with all the copper and tin that he needed, and he furiously demanded to see results.

Thus spurred, Cellini made a nine foot statue of Perseus in a mixture of sand and clay, mixed with animal hairs to give it body, and moulded around an iron framework. Over this, he built up a layer of wax as thick as the bronze would be in the finished statue. More clay and sand were put over this, and the whole lot was then baked for two days.

The heat hardened the clay and melted away the wax, leaving a mould into which the bronze could be poured. A pit was dug beside the furnace and the mould was buried in this, apart from openings at the top. Channels connected to these would carry the molten bronze from the furnace to the mould.

When told of the failure of the bronze to melt, Cellini rushed to the foundry and ranted at the workmen for their incompetence and stupidity.

Then came the arduous job of melting the metal, with all the drama that this entailed, and casting the statue. Two days after the casting had been completed, the mould was cool enough to be broken away. Inside it stood the gleaming bronze figure of Perseus, proudly holding aloft the head of the Medusa. It was wonderful but not yet as magnificent as Cellini wanted it to be. There were still imperfections that would have to be smoothed out with files, chisels or pumice stones. And gold leaf was to be applied as an added embellishment. Perseus's helmet and wings, his feet and a band across his chest were to shine with the glory of gold.

It took five years for all this work to be done. Then, on 27th April, 1554, the wondering watchers in the Piazza della Signoria in Florence, saw Cellini's masterpiece revealed in all its wonder.

And there it remained, delighting successive generations of citizens and tourists, until it was stored in vaults for safe keeping during the Second World War. After the war, a great foundryman, Bruno Bearzi, was given the job of repairing and replacing the statue. The statue's sword was steel which had become rusty, and part of its base was damaged.

While he was putting these things right, Bearzi decided to try to solve the mystery of Cellini's casting problems all those centuries earlier. He scraped off small portions of the metal and sent it away to be analysed. When the metallurgist's report came back, it showed that the Medusa base, which had been cast years before the figure of Perseus, was made of bronze of the usual constituency.

But when he came to look at the analysis of the contents of the Perseus figure, Bearzi had a surprise. Its bronze contained only 1·7 per cent tin, whereas it should have consisted of 10 per cent tin and 90 per cent copper.

Why was this? Cellini had received enough bronze and tin from the Duke to have made the statue of properly mixed bronze. But Cellini was an extravagant man, and whenever he had run into debt he seems to have taken what, for him, was the most obvious course. He had sold some of the Duke's costly tin to pay his creditors.

Immortality may have been what Cellini wanted. But, obviously, he was not willing to have this at any price. Not when he was being pursued by debtors who were no respecters of such a great genius as Benvenuto Cellini, goldsmith and sculptor extraordinary.

The only remaining piece of Cellini's work which can be attributed to him, is this salt cellar made for Francis the First of France.

The Unlucky Buccaneer

SAMUEL PEPYS, Secretary to the Admiralty, was holding a dinner party, not a particularly rare occurrence, as he was a man who was well known for his liking for good food and convivial company.

Pepys' guest of honour that evening was William Dampier, one of the most remarkable pirates of all time, if only for the reason that although he had spent most of his life as a rough sailor and rover, he had now become one of the most famous literary figures of his time.

When Dampier arrived at Pepys' house, he brought with him a copy of the book that had already made him famous, "A New Voyage", which was crammed with hitherto unknown information about far-away lands. Pepys' other guests had been expecting to meet a swaggering, arrogant sailor. They met instead a polite, soft-spoken man, with an unhappy brooding face, who looked as if he might be more at home in a solicitor's office rather than on the quarter-deck of a pirate vessel.

The truth of the matter was that Dampier's reputation as a pirate had been grossly overrated. He had never shown a genius for leadership, and he

When a mutiny broke out on a ship under his command, Dampier put the ringleaders in irons. This was an act which was to lead to his downfall.

---

had never been anything more than a fairly undistinguished member of the pirate brethren. If he had not become a famous literary figure, his sole claim to posterity would have been that a mutiny on one of his ships had led to the marooning of Alexander Selkirk on the island of Juan Fernandez. This gave Daniel Defoe the background for his book "Robinson Crusoe," in which he immortalized Selkirk for all time.

Dampier, had, nevertheless, led an exciting life. Born in the middle of the seventeenth century in a little village near Yeovil, he had gone to sea as a boy. From then, he had spent most of his life under sail, except for a brief period. Then he had become a businessman, running a logwood business in Jamaica. This ended when a tremendous hurricane swept across the Caribbean, destroying every ship in the area, and wiping out everything that Dampier owned.

The hurricane changed the lives of

hundreds of log cutters, who were mostly ex-buccaneers who had been forced to give up piracy since their one-time leader, Sir Henry Morgan, had been made Lieutenant-Governor of Jamaica. Now, with the lumber industry at a standstill, there was nothing they could do but to go back to their old trade of buccaneering. Dampier, with some misgivings, joined them.

His first venture at sea was typical of the way in which all his attempts at piracy seemed to be dogged with misfortune. Together with a party of pirates, he captured the town of Alvarado, near Vera Cruz in Mexico, only to find that all the inhabitants had already fled, taking with them their money and all the movable property of value.

After that, Dampier continued to rove the Spanish Main, occasionally capturing a Spanish vessel, but making little profit out of it. His life seemed to consist mostly of one fruitless raid after another, and desperate forced marches under various captains. The one thing with which he could console himself was that he had escaped from every battle without suffering a single scratch. Forced to walk across a dangerous and pestilent isthmus three times, he had emerged each time at the other end as hale and hearty as any man who had stayed comfortably at home by his own fireside.

Dampier had travelled around the world, surviving many perils and adventures before he returned to England, after an absence of twelve years. He had little more than the clothes he stood up in, and his only piece of "property" was a tattooed prince whom he had brought home in order to earn a living of sorts by exhibiting him at fairs. Before long, however, poverty forced Dampier to sell his prince to another, more business-like showman.

The one thing that eventually saved his fortunes was that he had succeeded in always keeping a diary in which he recorded everything he saw with extraordinary powers of observation. This was a remarkable feat for a common sailor who had always joined in the rough and ready life of his fellow-buccaneers who spent most of their time in drunken carousing. The diary became his famous book, "New Voyage Around the World". The book became a best seller, and as result of all the valuable information in it, the Admiralty made him a captain in the Royal Navy.

He was given the ship, "H.M.S. Roebuck", and was told to set off to explore New Holland, as Australia was then called. It was, like all of Dampier's ventures, an ill-fated voyage, thanks mostly to the efforts of his chief officer, a man named Fisher, who deliberately encouraged the crew to be insubordinate, merely because he deeply resented having to serve under a man who had been a buccaneer. A mutiny eventually broke out, which Dampier quickly resolved by putting the ring-leaders in irons. It was an act that was to ruin him.

Dampier managed to reach Australia without further incident, where he did a great deal of valuable exploration of the terrain. On his return trip, however, the ship sprang a leak and was just able to limp to the island of Ascension before it sank. All hands were saved, but for the next five weeks they kept themselves alive on bleak and barren Ascension Island on turtle meat and eggs.

When Dampier and his crew were finally rescued and taken home, Lieutenant Fisher immediately demanded that Dampier should be court-martialled for the way he had treated him.

Incredibly, Fisher won his case, and Dampier was judged an unfit person to be employed as a commander of any ship belonging to the royal fleet. Worse still, Dampier was fined all his pay.

Dampier's ill-luck dogged him to the very end. Unable to get another royal command, he sailed as pilot on a privateer under a Captain Woodes Rogers, who returned finally to England with Spanish spoils worth £200,000. Dampier died soon after landing, before the prize money was shared out.

Dampier nearly met his end when serving on a boat which had been so delayed by storms that the food had run out. The crew threatened to eat Dampier and the captain, but at the crucial moment land was sighted and they were saved.

The Mysterious Millionaire

High above the countryside the aeronauts gathered air samples. They did so at the request of Henry Cavendish, a rich scientist at work on theories years ahead of their time . . .

Throughout history there have been men who have seemingly been born ahead of their time, who were aware of possibilities that would not be fully realised until many centuries later. Such a man was the 18th century English scientist, Sir Henry Cavendish.

On November 30, 1784, Sir Henry Cavendish organised the first balloon ascent for scientific research. The aeronauts carried bottles filled with water which they emptied at predetermined altitudes, allowing them to fill up with air. Later Cavendish analysed this air: the first study of the composition of the atmosphere as a function of altitude.

In the air brought back by the aeronauts there were certain strange bubbles which were carefully collected by Cavendish. The bubbles were not composed of oxygen or nitrogen or any constituent of air. These so-called "noble gases" (argon, neon, helium) were not officially isolated until over a century later.

It is now known that Henry Cavendish was able to isolate these gases. In 1921 researchers discovered some trunks in one of Cavendish's laboratories. In these trunks were found test tubes filled with rare gases that Cavendish had studied by passing through them an electric charge.

Details of his research show that Cavendish had accurately determined the earth's mass and had calculated the deviation of light rays by the sun's mass, coming up with a result numerically very close to that which Einstein produced well over a century later.

On May 27, 1775, Cavendish had invited to his laboratories seven illustrious scientists to witness an experiment–an extraordinary experiment for that time. He produced an artificial electric-ray fish and gave the scientists electric shocks. Then Cavendish calmly informed his seven guests that this new force of electricity would change the world.

All Cavendish's knowledge was connected with alchemy (the chemistry of the middle ages) and Cavendish always used the alchemist's language and symbols, but his research has been and is being confirmed two centuries later by our most sophisticated science and our most advanced techniques.

Much of the work Cavendish devoted himself to in his various laboratories remains a mystery. There are several trunks of his hand-written papers which cannot at this time be understood and many scientific instruments whose use cannot yet be comprehended.

However, it is not only Cavendish's understanding of electricity, his isolation of rare gases and his many other amazingly anticipatory scientific researches that make this man so mysterious.

Sir Henry Cavendish was born in Nice in 1731 and died in Clapham, London, in 1810 (today the street where he lived is named after him). Although his childhood was poverty-stricken, throughout his adult life he appeared to be so rich that people believed he had achieved the alchemist's dream of turning base metal into gold!

It has never been explained just where his fortune came from. Every time someone brought him a list of contributions that had been made to various charities, Cavendish would hand over a sum equal to the highest figure paid! A student friend had financial problems and so Cavendish immediately sent him ten thousand pounds!

Cavendish kept up this extraordinary generosity throughout his life and yet when he died he left millions of pounds. He seems like the personification of the bottomless purse that we read about in the fairy tales!

Another mysterious fact about this man is that he was admitted to the Royal Academy of Science in 1760 at the unprecedented early age of twenty-nine. Not only had Cavendish no university degrees, he had not published a single scientific work.

The mysterious Henry Cavendish began in early middle age to act towards his fellows in a most surprising manner. As much as possible he tried to hide his face–and he hated to have anyone speak to him! If anyone, apart from a small circle of friends, spoke to him he would bow to the person, turn on his heel, order his carriage and promptly return home.

For thirty years until his death in 1810, he pursued a secret life. He went on mysterious trips into the country in a carriage which was equipped with a counter of his own invention–what this was for we cannot guess at but one is reminded of a modern taxi meter!

After his death his heirs examined his papers and discovered that he had been a principal stockholder of the Bank of England. *And yet Henry Cavendish had never earned anything in his life and had given away a fortune to charities.*

His will, which left his millions to his family, required that he was to be buried in a vault which was then to be immediately walled up. There was to be no inscription to indicate the tomb of the mysterious Henry Cavendish.

As he grew older, Cavendish's behaviour became more and more eccentric. If spoken to by someone other than a close friend, he would bow, turn on his heel and, entering his carriage, return home!

Masters Of Their Craft

Josiah Wedgwood (1730-95)

Brilliant technician, far-sighted industrial organiser, and superb craftsman: Josiah Wedgwood was all of these. Born in Staffordshire, he was the son of a potter, and apprenticed to his elder brother. An attack of smallpox threatened his career, for an infection led to the amputation of his right leg. Yet the period of disability proved a blessing, for he turned to reading, and this led to research and experiment which revolutionised the craft of pottery. He became potter to the queen, and in 1769 opened his Etruria works. Here he produced his most famous pieces, including the celebrated unglazed jasperware, with classical designs set in relief on a background of blue and other colours. The beautiful example pictured on the left is in the British Museum.

Antonio Stradivari (c. 1644-1737)

The dream of every budding violinist is one day to own a Stradivarius. For no violins have been made that quite match, in musical quality or appearance, the exquisite instruments designed and fashioned by the Italian craftsman Antonio Stradivari. He was born at Cremona, and in due course started to learn his trade from another famous maker, Nicolo Amati. As the years passed, and he set up on his own, Stradivari changed the traditional design of the instruments, making them longer and introducing the modern type of bridge and other improvements. He gave his products a beautiful finish with special varnish, the secret of which died with him. The best of his instruments were made in his later years, as in his younger days he could not afford the best materials.

Grinling Gibbons (1648-1721)

Most people know that it was Sir Christopher Wren who designed St. Paul's Cathedral, when it was built after the Great Fire of London in 1666. But not so many are aware that the imposing interior of this and many other Wren buildings owes much to the skill of stone and wood carver Grinling Gibbons. He had spent his childhood in the Netherlands, to which his father had emigrated, but came to England to practise his craft at Deptford. His success in decorating King Charles II's apartments at Windsor, and rooms in other royal palaces, established his reputation. His sculptures in stone included statues of King Charles and of his brother James II. But it is for his work in wood that Grinling Gibbons is chiefly celebrated. The floral design illustrated is typical of his marvellously delicate and graceful carving.

Thomas Tompion (c. 1639-1713)

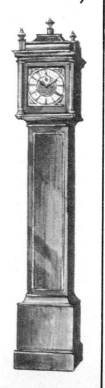

Wielding a blacksmith's hammer would seem to be no sort of preparation for the intricate business of fashioning watch and clock movements. But Thomas Tompion did start out as an apprentice in his father's forge in Bedfordshire. He soon abandoned this trade, and set up as a clockmaker in London. He took a close interest in new escapements (devices that control the mechanism of timepieces) then being introduced. He himself played a major part in developing them, producing one of the earliest hair-spring watches. Tompion, unlike many contemporaries, especially in France, concentrated his efforts on mechanical soundness and accuracy rather than elaborate decoration. His works included travelling and bracket clocks, "grandfather" clocks and chiming watches. Many of these survive, and keep good time to this day.

THE SPY WHO SAVED LONDON

ANYONE seeing him could tell at once what he was, a simple countryman unhurriedly making his way to work, carrying a small sack of potatoes in one hand and an axe in the other. From these two things, even the most simple-minded German soldier would have been able to deduce without too much trouble that he was a wood-cutter, and that the potatoes were probably for his lunch, which he would cook over an open fire.

Such a man was a common enough sight in this part of the country, and one could waste a great deal of time examining such people when one should be engaged in the more important business of guarding the Swiss frontier. It was true that spies trying to get over the border used all sorts of ruses and disguises, but invariably they did it far less openly than this man, and mostly they did it by night.

It was for these reasons that Michel Hollard, a French industrial designer turned spy, was left alone by the German patrols and Alsatian police dogs as he plodded steadily towards the frontier, carrying in the bottom of his sack a small piece of paper that was to prevent London from being totally destroyed.

The incredible story of Michel Hollard, which was inevitably kept secret until the end of the war, began when the Germans marched into Paris. As he stood on the pavement, his stony face masked his impotent anger as he watched the Germans goose-stepping through the streets of his beloved city. His bitter thoughts were not unlike those of most of his fellow countrymen. They were thoughts, however, which were to be crystallised into positive action when he learned that the company which employed him was preparing to work for the Germans. Indignantly, he resigned on the spot and

Hollard realised that the runway was not designed to carry ordinary aircraft and his compass showed that it pointed straight at London!

got himself a new job for a company which made charcoal gas burning generators. The reason he took this job was a very practical one. As a business man whose job it was to seek out wood for charcoal, he would have a ready made excuse for visiting the forests near the Swiss border. Mentally, Michel Hollard had already committed himself to his self-appointed mission— to help the Allies in every way he could to bring about the downfall of the Third Reich.

The way he chose to do this was to slip over the border into Switzerland, where he offered his services as a spy to the British. On their behalf he identified German troop units and reported their movements. Always he worked alone, without the benefit of an official network, crossing and recrossing the border whenever he had any information to impart. Despite the lack of any official backing, he eventually built up a large network of his own, consisting of one hundred and twenty loyal Frenchmen recruited from all walks of life. Al-

though twenty of them were eventually captured and put to death, this loss was a relatively small one compared to some of the networks directly under the control of the British.

It was Hollard's network which led him to track down the plans of the V-I, a pilotless explosive rocket with which Hitler intended to reduce London to ruins. The first inkling Hollard had that something very sinister was afoot was via a report from one of his agents. While this man had been sitting in a cafe in Rouen, he had overheard two building contractors discussing some unusual construction work that was being done in the area by the Germans. Hollard immediately went to Rouen. Here, by dint of a number of cautious enquiries, he managed to find out that a great number of workers were labouring round the clock on a site outside the town of Auffay.

He arrived at the site the same day, now dressed in blue overalls. Mingling with the workers, he seized a wheelbarrow and trundled it towards a long stretch of concrete not unlike a short runway. Surreptitiously using a compass, he worked out that the strip was pointing directly towards London.

Hollard was in a thoughtful mood when he left the site. It was no coincidence surely that the runway pointed in the direction of London. As it was clearly no runway for an ordinary plane, did this mean that what he had just seen was some sort of missile launching pad? And if it were, what sort of missile were the Germans going to launch from it? Perhaps an even more important question was, were there more such bases dotted around that part of France? There was only one way to find the answer to that question. A few days later, Hollard and four of his agents, all equipped with maps and mounted on bicycles,

began a systematic tour of the area.

Several weeks later they compared notes and found that between them they had discovered no less than a hundred similar sites, all of which pointed in the direction of London. Their next problem was to find out what the Germans were eventually going to launch from them.

Fortunately for Hollard, an incredible stroke of luck was about to supply him with someone who was in the position to deliver Hitler's best kept secret into his hands. The person in question was a young man named Andre, who was already working as one of his agents was moved on to another job—on one of the rocket sites. Andre was a patriotic Frenchman who had already done useful work, but he jibbed at first at the next assignment that Hollard gave him—that of stealing the master plans for that particular site. This was a very hazardous mission as the overseer kept the plan in his overcoat most of the time. Nevertheless, a copy of the plan was in Hollard's possession within the next few days.

The next step was for Hollard to get the plan over the Swiss border and into the hands of the British. It was for that reason that a seemingly innocent woodcutter happened to be wandering through the woods near the Swiss border on that cold misty October morning in 1943.

Hollard had actually got as far as the viciously spiked rolls of barbed wire when he heard a terrible growl behind him. The next moment he was brought down by a large German police dog which promptly seized hold of one of his legs with all the joyous relish of an animal taking hold of a succulent bone.

Desperately Hollard groped around for a stick with which to beat of the fierce German guard dog.

Hollard had already thrown his axe and the sack of potatoes over the wire, so he had nothing with which he could beat off the dog. Reaching about him wildly, his groping hand fastened on a large stick which he thrust between the animal's jaws, until he managed to get it down the windpipe. Tenaciously, the dog continued to hold on to his leg. Then quite suddenly it rolled over dead.

As he began to wriggle between the coils of wire he could hear the sound of voices shouting in German behind him. Reaching the other side of the wire, he found himself confronted with a Swiss guard with a raised rifle. He was, however, not pointing it at Hollard, but at the two German soldiers who were levelling their rifles at Hollard. Seeing that the Swiss guard was quite prepared to shoot them if necessary, the Germans turned away and disappeared into the woods. Hollard gratefully reported to the Swiss guard post, and then in due course delivered to the British the plan of the weapon that could have well brought London to her knees.

Soon afterwards, Allied bombers began attacking the V-I emplacements. In all, they completely destroyed or put out of action seventy three of the sites. Others were built, and London was still subjected to a certain amount of bombardment from the V-I's. But Hitler's master plan to destroy the city by raining down fifty thousand bombs, had been shattered.

A further happy note to the story of the man who saved London from complete destruction is that he survived the war, even though he was later captured and tortured by the Germans, before being sent to a concentration camp. Surviving all this, he was flown back by the R.A.F. to London, where he was decorated with the Distinguished Service Order.

Ask Me Another

1. What is lapis lazuli?
2. What is insomnia?
3. Who wrote the opera "Faust"?
4. The members of which religion are bound by the following five rules of conduct: no living being is to be killed; no one is to take what has not been given him; adultery is strictly forbidden; no man is to utter an untruth; all intoxicating drinks are to be avoided?
5. To which animal family does the buffalo belong?
6. Which is the largest and deepest-toned of the woodwind instruments?
7. For which annual event is Henley-on-Thames famous?
8. On what and how do frogs feed?
9. For what reason is the Quaker Elizabeth Fry remembered?
10. Who discovered that a wire carrying an electric current is surrounded by a magnetic field?
11. Who was the King of Assyria about whom Lord Byron wrote an epic poem?
12. Tom Sawyer, Mark Twain's mischievous hero, lived in the town of St. Petersburg on the Mississippi. What town did Twain use as the model for St. Petersburg?
13. Who, in 1870, discovered the ancient city of Troy?
14. On a plaque outside St. Paul's Church in London's Covent Garden is the inscription: "Near this spot Punch's Puppet Show was first performed in England–1662." Who brought Mr. Punch to England?
15. The forked tongue of the grass snake is not used for stinging. What is its use?
16. Which is Britain's smallest native duck?
17. To which place did Jesus go to pray after the Last Supper?
18. Who were the first two disciples called by Jesus?
19. What was the trade of these two men?
20. When did India become a self-governing Dominion of the British Commonwealth?

NOW TURN TO PAGE 127 FOR THE ANSWERS

The City of Discoveries

WOODEN clogs go clumping up the steep streets. Hoarse voices, shrill and strident, echo between the houses that line the winding thoroughfares.

"Fish for sale. Fresh from the sea. Come and buy it."

The cry of the fish women of Lisbon grows louder and then fades away into the distance as the women, baskets of fish on their heads, go about their job of selling their wares to the café proprietors, hoteliers and housewives of one of Europe's most ancient capitals, Lisbon, the seat of Portugal's government.

It is a cry which is as old as the city itself—and as unchanging. Governments may come and go. Riots and revolutions may disturb the surface calm. Tanks and sieges . . . the newspapers have had a stormy story to tell about Lisbon in recent years.

But while revolution may have seethed beneath the surface, and finally burst into life like a volcano, Lisbon—the real Lisbon behind the shop fronts and the cafés—remains much as it has been for generation after generation.

Above the broad, blue waters of the River Tagus rise terraces of tall, white houses, their windows protected by striped awnings from the hot sun. The melancholy song of a

The streets of Lisbon resound to the cries of the fisherwomen as they go about the task of selling their wares.

In 1755 a terrible earthquake, followed by a tidal wave and a fire, caused immense damage to the city. Below: for those who like the thrill of a bullfight, Lisbon offers two rings. The Portuguese do not kill the bull, the object of the contest being to bring the creature to a standstill.

fado or gipsy singer drifts from a café across the crowded sunny square.

Washing dangles in the breeze, strung high between plaster walls. And among the crowds, wandering still, are the fisherwomen, or *varinas*, their baskets of fish lighter now, for sales have been brisk.

Lisbon is one of the loveliest cities in Europe. Its magnificent squares, churches, palaces and convents are built on a series of low, green hills above the harbour of the Tagus, which provides a vast seaport for ocean-going liners, Portuguese fishing boats and tourists' yachts alike.

Lisbon is a noisy, bustling capital. The picturesque, medieval quarter of the old lower town is always crammed with people, jostling up and down streets which twist steeply between pink and white houses, ornate stucco churches and dark shops.

The old town, with its inevitable lines of washing, is crowned by the Moorish fortress of St. George, where white peacocks strut along the battlements. Above this and to the west lies the more recent quarter of spacious streets, squares, parks and busy shopping centres.

Little of this part of the city dates back before 1755. In that year, a terrible earthquake shook Lisbon, followed by a tidal wave and a fire in which thousands of citizens perished. Nearly every street had to be repaired or reconstructed.

Now, the fashionable residents of Lisbon can stroll along the broad Avenida da Liberdade with its fountains or double rows of trees, or watch the waters of the Tagus flow past from the side of Black Horse Square, where the great equestrian statue of King Joseph I stands. They can go to one of two bull-rings and see the Portuguese *tourada*, in which the toreador, on a spirited horse, teases the bull and expertly dodges his horns. Then come the bullfighters who taunt the bull and finally wrestle it to a standstill. With this, the fight is over, and the bull is led from the ring to fight another day.

After watching the spectacle in

the arena, visitors can go to one of the innumerable cafés. Most of these are filled with men drinking coffee, reading or having their shoes blacked, for women seldom visit cafés with men.

Often, the only woman in a café is the *fado* singer, clad in her traditional black shawl, pouring out a harsh, throbbing lament to the sound of two guitars. When the customers want another coffee or another song they do not call for the waiter. Instead, they hiss, for hissing is polite in Lisbon.

Then the melancholy notes of the *fado* singer begin again. *Fado*, translated, means "fate", and there is a sadness in this national singing which sounds like the soul of the people lamenting it knows not what.

Many of Lisbon's visitors arrive at the busy airport, which is linked by jet with London, Madeira, Las Palmas and the Azores islands. Others arrive by water, seeing, as they sail towards Lisbon's pastel painted houses clinging to the hillsides, a city that is homely, rambl-

ing and picturesque. Many make their way to the terrace of the old Moorish fort of St. George, which overlooks the whole city and the river.

From the fort, you can see the steep, twisting streets of the old city, the wide avenues laid out by the Marquis of Pombal after the 1755 earthquake, and the modern flats and shops of the suburbs towards the airport in the west.

A short journey takes you to the point of the north bank of the River Tagus near Lisbon on which stands a monument to the famous seamen of Portugal.

Portugal has always been a seafaring nation. For 33 years, from 1487 to 1520, the seamen, the navigators and chart makers of Portugal were dominant in Europe. They reached as far east as Japan,

Henry the Navigator was the inspiration behind many great voyages of discovery. Explorers setting out from Lisbon discovered a great deal about the coast of Africa and even ventured as far as Abyssinia.

as far west as Brazil. About one-third of the then known world was Portuguese-discovered. Vasco da Gama, Corte Real, Alvarex Cabral, Bartolomeu Dias, Ferdinand Magellan—this is a roll call of salty mariners carrying the flag of Portugal about the Seven Seas.

Perhaps the greatest of them all was Prince Henry the Navigator, son of King John I and his English queen, Philippa, daughter of John of Gaunt. Henry was a map-maker, an explorer, to whom the world presented an infinity of discovery starting with Madeira and ranging as far as Abyssinia. He equipped endless expeditions, each one carried out by fully-trained men.

The monument which commemorates Portugal's era of exploration is called the Monument of Discoveries, and it was built in 1960 to mark the 500th anniversary of the death of Henry the Navigator. Lisbon also has a connection with Christopher Columbus who learned about map-making and astronomy there and made his first journeys in Portuguese ships.

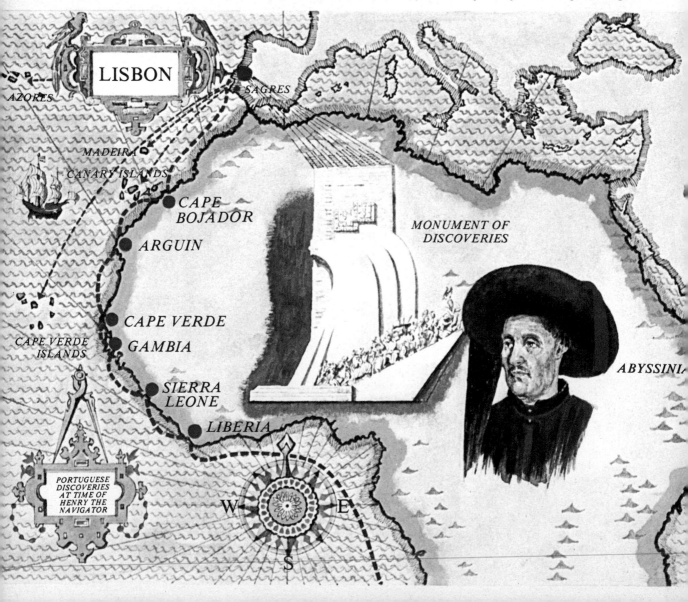

AZORES

LISBON

SAGRES

MADEIRA

CANARY ISLANDS

CAPE BOJADOR

ARGUIN

CAPE VERDE

GAMBIA

CAPE VERDE ISLANDS

SIERRA LEONE

LIBERIA

MONUMENT OF DISCOVERIES

ABYSSINIA

PORTUGUESE DISCOVERIES AT TIME OF HENRY THE NAVIGATOR

W   E

S

PETS FOR POTENTATES

Rulers in the past have had some exotic and unusual creatures to keep them company.

"ABUL ABBAS is dead," the dread whisper spread down the palace corridors.

"What will the Emperor say? Will he be angry?" asked others in trembling fear.

"How will we bury Abul Abbas?" asked some. And how indeed do you bury a dead elephant? Naturally the Emperor Charlemagne was upset that his elephant had died. In the 8th century Abul Abbas had been the only elephant in Europe and Charlemagne, Emperor of the Franks, was very proud of him.

Abul Abbas was in fact a gift from one great potentate to another, from Harun al Rashid the Caliph of Baghdad to the greatest Christian ruler of Western Europe. This elephant became the most popular animal in France and when at last the chilly climate of the north killed poor Abul Abbas the chroniclers noted this sad fact in their histories of the time.

This was the so-called Dark Ages after the Western half of the Roman Empire had collapsed. Now the

Even after her death the Empress of China's dogs were faithful and attacked soldiers who looted her tomb.

power, the money and the exotic animals were held by the sultans and caliphs of the Middle East. Theirs really was an Arabian Nights world, and while they might send one ordinary elephant to their barbarous European neighbours they kept the best for themselves.

Take Zureyk the blue-eyed lion for example. He was the pampered pet of Sultan Khumaraweyh who ruled the glittering city of Cairo some years after poor old Abul Abbas had died. Khumaraweyh's story comes straight out of those fantastic Arabian Nights tales—yet it was true. This sultan suffered from insomnia and so he would try to doze on an air-bed floating in a pool of quicksilver, listening to tame turtle-doves in the trees while Zureyk his blue-eyed lion lay in a nearby bed of roses to guard his master.

Naturally lions were always popular with those potentates who fancied themselves as masters of the world. The Romans were particularly prone to the King of Beasts. Prestige was important in those days (things haven't changed much!) and some Emperors tried to impress their subjects by pretending to be the god-like masters of wild animals. When Mark Antony got back from defeating Pompey he gave the Romans a real show, driving down the Via Triumphalis in a chariot drawn by lions which roared at the cowering crowd. Somewhere in the background, of course, Mark Antony's lion tamer stood ready just to be sure

Whilst the Sultan Khumaraweyh dozed, his blue eyed lion kept guard.

that Rome's new hero did not make a hash of it.

Caracalla was another soldier who grabbed the dangerous throne of Caesar. He developed the habit of sleeping with a tame lion at the bottom of his bed. It didn't save him of course. When Caracalla decided to conquer Persia his generals murdered him just before he led his army off into the eastern deserts–though they had to kill the faithful lion first.

Another rather odd Emperor, Elegabalus, took things even further. He locked lions in the banqueting hall with some drunken, overfed guests who were sleeping off the previous night's party. Perhaps they considered this too drastic a way of curing a hang-over, for they got rid of Elegabalus a short while later–permanently!

SACRED CATS

Claudius was different. Apart from being a bit of a bookworm he had a thing about tigers. This Emperor used to keep four of them in his room at night.

The feline family was also popular in Iran, but there the Shah and his nobles had more style than those pompous Romans. They liked small cats, not big ones. The leading nobles of that ancient land used to keep sacred Egyptian temple cats as pets. Then along came Alexander the Great and his Greeks to carve up the Persian Empire. Some of Persia's defeated warlords retreated with their families and followers into the mountains of Khorasan, and trotting beside them went the faithful temple cats. In Khorasan these cats shared Iran's long and savage resistance to the Greeks until eventually their descendants followed the Iranian warriors back down from the wind-swept valleys of Khorasan to drive the invaders out of their

At a signal from their master the canaries would join in the music.

land. But these cats were now different. Their ancestors, the Egyptian temple cats, had mated with the long-haired wild cats of Khorasan and their offspring turned out to have the longest hair of all. The first proud Persian Cats had been born.

Generally speaking dogs have been lower down the social scale than cats, and few can claim Imperial connections. The lion-dogs of Peking are an exception. According to legend they are descended from a lion and a marmoset who fell in love long ago in the forests of Korea. But a lion is big while a marmoset is very small. Fortunately the lion's love was so great that a wise old Buddhist hermit who lived nearby was able to shrink the King of Beasts down to a marmoset's size. That's why, they say, the Pekinese dog is as small as a marmoset but as brave as a lion.

Some British and French soldiers who burst into the Forbidden City of Peking back in 1860 found that out for themselves. These invaders, looking for loot, discovered the body of the old Empress of China lying behind a delicate bamboo curtain in her Palace. But as one soldier stepped into the room he was attacked by five little flat-faced dogs. These were the Imperial Pekes, determined to defend their Empress's body.

Indeed they had the lion's courage, but the marmoset's size let them down. They too were carted off as spoils of war. One was given the name "Looty" before being presented to Queen Victoria. This proud Peke at least spent the rest of his life in a Royal Court, so he can't have been too offended.

Some other dogs can claim to be members of the upper crust–greyhounds for example. Their ancestors were the hunting dogs of the Egyptian pharaohs, and until quite recently the sheikhs of the Arabian desert considered a greyhound far too fine to sell. They would only give them away!

Giving animals as gifts or bribes has been going on

For some Roman citizens the sounds made by trained apes was music to their ears!

for some time. Egypt was declining fast when Rameses IX came to the throne, but although he had a weak army Rameses also had a great zoo. Instead of fighting the warrior Assyrians, and probably getting massacred in the process, the pharaohs sent his neighbour a whole selection of monkeys, crocodiles and hippos to keep him quiet.

Of course Egypt's rulers had been building up their collection for hundreds of years. Around 1490 B.C. Queen Hatshepsut sent a naval expedition to the fabled land of Punt somewhere down in East Africa. She gave admiral Nehsi strict instructions to bring back any interesting creatures he found, and he brought baboons as is shown on a carving in Queen Hatshepsut's temple.

Rome's rulers took this monkey business a stage further, training Barbary Apes to play musical instruments and wear the kind of clothes that fat Roman aristocrats wore at feasts. They must have made a ghastly din, though perhaps no worse than some of those Romans who thought themselves such marvellous musicians.

ROYAL AUDIENCE

King Louis XIV of France was luckier. Monsieur de Chanteloup's Canary Concerts were all the rage among the fashionable ladies of the Court, especially when the King deigned to witness this extraordinary spectacle. While flute, oboe and shawm tootled from one corner of the room, a wave of Monsieur's wand would set rows of yellow canaries echoing the music. The more talented birds were even trained to dance. The star of this show was named "Monsieur Lully" because Chanteloup was convinced that his extraordinary canary was a reincarnation of that famous French composer. "Monsieur Lully" also danced—until he broke his leg. They

As he examined the wounded heron, Frederick made a startling discovery.

The falcon thought the old heron would be an easy prey—but he soon learnt otherwise.

then gave the bird a wooden one, so at least he could still sing.

Other potentates preferred pigeons. Akhbar the Great of India was a fanatical pigeon fancier. He set up the best pigeon postal service the world had seen. He also had an elite squadron of birds that were trained to fly in formation, loop, dive and zoom in obedience to whistled commands.

Sadly when such stars of the animal kingdom came up against kings, potentates and princes they lost their independence and became mere pets. One exception is, however, recorded. This was a heron. One day back in the 1750s the Elector Frederick of Saxony went out hawking with his squires. He set his favourite falcon at a heron, but every time the bird of prey swooped upon its victim the old heron rose to meet its attacker with its sharp beak lifted to pierce the falcon's blood-crazed heart.

Finally the falcon did make a strike, latching on to the heron's shoulder like a leech as both birds tumbled to earth. The Elector of Saxony was now so excited that he scrambled through the heather to where the birds had fallen.

"God's Blood," Frederick muttered as he knelt beside the wounded heron, "there are two silver rings on the bird's leg. See, this ring bears my name for here is the brave heron we caught ten years ago. Look! The other ring bears the seal of the Sultan of Turkey. This heron was also brought down by the Sultan's own hawk outside Constantinople."

So the brave bird was cared for, fed, ringed yet again and then released. Such blood-sports were cruel, although of course most birds were hunted for food as well as for fun. Nevertheless in those days men seemed to have a certain respect for the courage and dignity of the animal kingdom; a respect which all too often we seem to have lost.

Hang Gliding

THE SPORT THAT'S TAKING OFF

LAUNCH yourself off the side of a hill or a mountain–and away you go. Over fields and rivers you soar, to land with a bump in a field of thistles among a herd of astonished cows.

"It's all part of the game," you tell yourself, as you clamber to your feet and trudge up the hill, taking with you the kite that had carried you like a bird over hill and dale.

An experience like this is all part of the sport of hang gliding which is both thrilling and dangerous. It is thrilling because the flyers enjoy a wonderful feeling of elation and freedom as they float along. Coupled with this is the moment of fear which comes just before the take-off, for they know that their kites could crash. Sometimes a kite *does* crash, and the result is a broken limb or even death.

Hang gliders began from an idea evolved by an American, Dr. Francis Rogalla, in 1950. He designed a glider that he hoped could be used to bring space capsules back to Earth after they had returned from orbit.

However, the Americans preferred to use parachutes for this job. Excitement-seekers saw in Dr. Rogalla's kite the germ of a new sport. Now they sail through the sky while sitting or lying on a trapeze suspended under a nylon kite rigged on a tubular metal framework. To guide their kite, they simply move their body from side to side. This action moves strings attached to the controls.

Thousands of people in Britain, America and the Continent go hang gliding. The British ones belong to the British Hang Gliding Association, which approves the kites. Schools have been set up to teach the theory of flight and to introduce pupils to flying in two-man kites. Clubs are being formed where beginners can learn the technique of gliding.

The gliders' frames are made of heat-treated aluminium alloy and the sails of strengthened nylon. Because the gliders only weigh about 19 kilos (42 lbs) they can be carried on car roof racks. In light winds of 25 km. (16 mph), it is possible to achieve long soaring flights, even as long as eight hours in exceptional circumstances. A skilled pilot can manoeuvre his glider so skilfully that he can bring it to rest on a target many miles away from the jumping off point.

Hang gliding did not develop as a sport until late in 1971 when a Californian discovered the technique of ridge soaring–staying aloft for as long as you wish. This is made possible by steering the nylon sailwing from the triangle of aluminium tubing suspended underneath. Depending upon the conditions and their skill, gliders can stay airborne for periods varying from minutes to hours.

And when they land, the pilots are filled with a mixture of joy and relief, ready to answer "Yes" to the fellow pilot who calls encouragingly, "Shall we go back up to the top of the hill and try again?"

Before any flight, the long trek to the top of a hill is necessary. When the kite is in flight it is guided by simple movements of the body.

RECORD BREAKERS AT
BROOKLANDS

TREES grow through the cracks in the concrete. Straggling weeds and moss flourish where once the giants of the world of speed roared around the banked turns. Brooklands motor racing track, where John Cobb hit the heights of speed with 151.97 mph in the years between the wars, sleeps today.

Once one of the world's most famous tracks, Brooklands was sold to Vickers-Armstrong in 1946 and became an aircraft factory.

But memories of its fame will remain undimmed in the minds of those who will never forget its importance in the growth of motor racing.

Its story began in 1906 when a motor fan, H. F. Locke-King, went to a motor race in Italy and found not a single British competitor there.

When he returned to England, Locke-King decided to put this matter right. He consulted a friend, who was a railway engineer, and together they planned a racing circuit, a feature

Farms and a factory were sacrificed and a river was bridged to prepare the site for the Brooklands racing track.

of which was to be banked bends to increase the lap speeds.

The setting they chose for their track was Weybridge in Surrey. Calling in another friend, Colonel Holden, they said, in effect, "Here's a piece of swampy, wooded land, Turn it into a super speedway."

To clear the land for the track meant buying a couple of farms and running bridges over the River Wey at two points. It also involved clearing away a small factory and putting solid foundations on land that was sandy and unstable.

However, plans were drawn up and passed and work on the site began in the autumn of 1906. On to the rural community descended battalions of workmen – 1,500 of them – bringing vast numbers of railway lines and sleepers to be used in the building process.

A great area of woodland had to be cleared, the route of a

In one of the inter-war races at Brooklands, Austin Dobson in the bi-motor Alfa Romeo (above right) and John Cobb in a Napier Railton battle it out.

Mechanics in the pits service a car during a Brooklands meeting. Checks are made on such points as tyres, oil levels and fuel before the car goes back into the race.

After the outbreak of the Second World War, Brooklands' racing days were ended and the site was used for the manufacture of such aircraft as the Wellington bomber (above, right), seen being manhandled over a bridge spanning the River Wey. Below: the track today, with weeds growing through the cracked concrete.

river changed, and a seemingly non-stop sequence of legal actions had to be contested.

Agreements had to be made with local councils and private citizens, and ways had to be found of housing the great army of workmen.

In June, 1907, the track was finally ready for use. Its official opening was on 17th June when the track was declared to be the eighth wonder of the world.

To the enthusiasts of that time, this description must have seemed apt. It consisted of two circuits, one of 3½ miles (5.6 km.) and the other of 2 miles (3.2 km.) And the width of the track was a hundred feet (30.4 m.) which made it suitable for the largest and fastest cars then available.

Two weeks after the opening, Brooklands was the scene of a world record attempt. A racing star of those days, S. F. Edge, decided to make an attempt on the 24 hour record, then held by an American who had covered 800 miles in this time.

Edge in his 60 hp Napier was out to average 60 mph to reach a total mileage of 1,440. The pessimists doubted whether he could do it, but Edge roared around the track, breaking one track record after another.

By night, a row of hurricane lamps around the middle of the track gave him a course to follow, and during the day he followed a line of paint daubs which had been put there to guide him.

Edge kept going and, after the 24 hour deadline had been passed, had driven over 1,581 miles for an average speed of just under 66 mph, a record which no other competitor was able to surpass for 17 years.

This achievement brought Brooklands into the full publicity limelight, and crowds made their way to the track for the first public meeting on 6th July.

At this meeting, the racing was fairly good, the first race being won by H. C. Tryon driving Edge's Napier. But there was a great deal of disappointment about the way the track was organised. But the shortcomings were overcome and, by the end of the season, the track was getting into its stride.

Public attention was focused on Brooklands again when Felice Nazarro skimmed around the track in an outsize Fiat at the amazing speed of 121.64 mph.

Attendances at the meetings improved and motor racing was rapidly becoming a flourishing spectator sport when, in 1914, the First World War broke out.

A feature of Brooklands had been an aerodrome contained within its boundaries, and many of the early flyers had taken off from here. The government commandeered the track and the aerodrome, but only used the aerodrome. Many of the famous flyers who battled in the air against the German pilots in this war were based at Brooklands.

With the end of the war, motor racing came into its own again. The first post-war meeting took place on 24th May, 1920.

The growth of the motor industry made vast crowds aware of the spectacular excitement provided by motor racing, and Brooklands was at the peak of its fame.

It took a Second World War and changes in the pattern of motor racing to bring about Brooklands' demise in 1946—a sad end to an exciting chapter in the history of sport.

But this may not be the end of the story of Brooklands. A band of enthusiasts are trying to get at least part of the track re-opened as a living transport museum in which veteran racers can recreate the pioneering days of the past.

Some of the famous names of Brooklands with their cars. Top: John Cobb and his Napier Railton. Middle: Prince Bira and his Maserati. Bottom: Raymond Mays and his ERA.

The Loser Who Became A Legend

THE council of war had been held aboard the supply steamer, "Far West", moored on the Yellowstone River, deep in the Montana wilderness. The plan of campaign decided upon had been simple. It was known that the hostile Sioux under Sitting Bull were somewhere between the Rosebud and the Big Horn rivers, so the forces of Generals Terry and Gibbon would march up the Big Horn while the 7th Cavalry under Lieutenant Colonel Custer would move up the Rosebud. The two columns should wait until the other was in position and then, acting as an anvil and sledgehammer, they would crush the Sioux in the middle.

This was the intention, the plan of campaign...

Noon, 22nd June, 1876. The 7th Cavalry were ready to move out. Some six hundred tough, weather-beaten men, their uniforms ragged and stained after a month's hard riding, each man carrying with him all the bulky equipment needed for a field campaign–bedding roll lashed behind saddle cantle, canteen, haversacks, single-shot Springfield carbine and Colt revolver, extra rounds of ammunition. They rode

proudly, these men, for they were "the Fighting 7th" and they could handle anything they met. In perfect formation, in columns of four, they rode by, guidons fluttering and twelve buglers playing "Garry-owen", the 7th's battle song.

As the last troop and its train of pack mules passed by, Lieutenant Colonel Custer, resplendent in a tailored buckskin jacket and wide-brimmed white hat, wheeled about his prancing horse and took his leave of Generals Terry and Gibbon.

"Now, Custer", reminded Gibbon, "there are Indians enough for all of us. Don't be greedy–wait for us!"

Custer looked back, smiling. "No, I won't!" he called out, waving his gauntleted hand.

With that enigmatic reply, Custer spurred his horse and cantered after the column to take his place at the head of his regiment, leaving Terry and Gibbon to wonder what he had meant...

George Armstrong Custer first made his name as a cavalry leader in the American Civil War. Although he had graduated from the Military Academy of West Point bottom of his class with a record number of demerits against him, it was not long before he was appointed a brigadier general of volunteers in command of the Michigan Cavalry Brigade.

It was no wonder that this twenty-three-year-old general –the American press nicknamed him the "boy general"– caught the imagination of the public and became a popular hero. A born showman, affecting flamboyant uniforms of his own design, and one of the finest horsemen in the U.S. Army, he cut a splendid figure standing just under six foot with golden hair falling in curls to broad shoulders.

At the end of the Civil War, the volunteer service being disbanded, Custer reverted to his regular army rank of captain (although he continued to be addressed as "General" by his officer friends). In 1866 he was promoted to lieutenant colonel and assigned to the newly-formed 7th Cavalry.

Ten years later, on 17th May, 1876, Lieutenant Colonel Custer at the head of the 7th Cavalry left his headquarters, Fort Abraham Lincoln, on campaign against Sitting Bull's Sioux.

For more than five weeks, Custer and the 7th had been riding towards the Little Big Horn; weary, unkempt, dust-coated men and horses. It was the morning of 25th June when they rode through a large, abandoned Indian camp. . . .

Unknown to the 7th Cavalry, here at this spot just three weeks before, Sitting Bull had danced the Sun Dance and seen the greatest vision of his life. After dancing all day, facing the sun from its rising to its setting, and all night until noon of the following day, the Bull had fallen to the ground in a faint and dreamed a vision of many blue-coated soldiers falling upside-down from the sky right into the Indian camp.

News of Sitting Bull's vision had spread fast and, by 25th June, the largest concentration of Indians ever to assemble in one place was camped on the banks of the Little Big Horn River which the Indians knew as the Greasy Grass. Sitting Bull's Huncpapa Sioux had been joined now by the Ogalallas, Minniconjous, Sans Arcs, Two Kettles, Yanktonais, Santees, Brules and the Cheyennes and Arapahoes, more than half armed with rifles of a better quality than those of the soldiers. They waited for the prophecy of victory over the bluecoats to be fulfilled.

By late morning of 25th June, the 7th Cavalry were almost upon the Indian camp, but still Custer did not comprehend the magnitude of the Indian force despite repeated warnings from his scouts. The one thought uppermost in his mind was that the cavalry column had been seen by the Indians and he must

attack at once or they would get away. There was no thought of waiting for Generals Terry and Gibbon.

Now the time had come for action and Custer was in his element, his blue eyes flashing with excitement. In the heat of this June morning he had discarded his buckskin jacket and was now dressed simply in a blue flannel shirt, buckskin trousers and high boots. The Indians were not to recognise "Long Hair" Custer this day for he had had his hair trimmed short for this campaign.

In order to cut off the Indian's retreat, Custer split his command into three. Captain Benteen was ordered to lead three companies to the west of the village and Major Reno and three companies were to cross the Little Big Horn River and

George Armstrong Custer.

charge the Indian camp from the south. Custer with five companies was to attack from the north. It was high noon.

Reno and his one hundred and fifty men rode about three miles down the Little Big Horn valley when they were met by hordes of mounted, yelling Indian warriors. Reno retreated to the bluffs on the opposite side of the river. Here his seriously-depleted force was rescued by the opportune arrival of Captain Benteen and his three companies.

It now seemed clear that the Indians were not trying to run away!

From their defensive position on the bluffs, surrounded by hundreds of Sioux and Cheyenne, Reno and Benteen heard heavy firing far down in the valley and they knew that their commander was engaged in battle—but there was no way

they could get through the Indians to aid him.

The Indians laid siege to the bluffs until late the next day, 26th June, when, unexpectedly, they withdrew. At sunset the soldiers could see the mighty forces of the Sioux and Cheyenne moving majestically southwards, away from the scene of their greatest victory.

Early the next morning, 27th June, the troops of Generals Terry and Gibbon came up the river from the north and discovered the fate of Custer and his five companies. *The only living thing to be found was Captain Keogh's horse, Comanche.*

On that terrible hillside the bodies of some two hundred soldiers lay where they had fought and died. At the summit, Custer's body was found. He had been shot in the temple and in the left side. Unlike most of his command, Custer had not been scalped or mutilated.

Custer and his two hundred men had found themselves surrounded by some two thousand mounted Indians and Custer had grouped his men back to back for a final stand.

Severely handicapped by their defective Springfield carbines—the spent cartridge would jam when the rifle was overheated and it had to be worked out with a knife—these men fought valiantly against tremendous odds.

According to one Indian participant the fight on "Custer Hill", as it is now called, lasted "for as long as it takes a white man to eat dinner" and, as Sitting Bull himself was to say later, "These men who came with the 'Long Hair' were as good men as ever fought."

The American public was shaken by the news of the "Custer Massacre": of the six hundred officers and men of the 7th Cavalry who fought at the Little Big Horn, two hundred and sixty five were dead and fifty two wounded. A scapegoat had to be found and one was at hand in the shape of Major Reno. He was branded a coward for failing to come to Custer's aid.

The defeat at the Little Big Horn conferred upon "General" Custer of the 7th Cavalry an immortality and fame that he could never have achieved with the greatest of victories. When Custer and his two hundred men rode down into that hot, dusty valley, they rode into legend.

Battle Against An Unseen Enemy

NOBODY suspected that danger—even death—lurked within the antiseptic surroundings of a hospital, when a man and woman called to visit a sick patient.

They did not know—nobody knew—that the young woman in the bed next to their friend

In Ethiopia, the United Nations medical teams visit outlying areas in search of the dreaded killer disease, smallpox.

was a smallpox victim. She was a technician and had been helping to develop a strain of smallpox at the London School of Hygiene and Tropical Medicine.

While doing this, she had become infected. But, because smallpox is so rare in Britain it was not discovered until after the woman had been admitted to hospital and tests were made to identify her disease. Once it was known that she had smallpox, she was rushed to an isolation hospital.

But, before this had happened, she had unwittingly passed on the disease to the two people visiting the patient in the next bed. After the disease had been identified and all the known contacts traced, it was too late to save the unfortunate couple – they were dead.

This was a rare event in Britain where smallpox is an almost unheard of disease. It may soon be as rare in the rest of the world if the work of the World Health Organisation in carrying out wholesale vaccination against the disease bears fruit.

Edward Jenner (above) achieved a victory for himself, and all mankind, when he found the answer to the smallpox scourge. It is easy to imagine his joy when visiting his child patient to discover that his vaccination of the boy had been successful.

A few years ago, two-and-a-half million people were dying every year from smallpox, which was a terror disease in thirty countries. However, the mass vaccination programme paid off and the disease remained rampant in only two countries – Ethiopia and Bangladesh. A big onslaught was made upon it and it was hoped that in due course the world would be completely free of smallpox.

In Ethiopia, the disease was tackled by teams of United Nations doctors and nurses. They toured the country in Land Rovers. Wherever they stopped, curious children would inevitably crowd around the medical team and their vehicle.

Clambering out of the vehicle, one of the doctors would show the children two posters. One was of a baby and the other was of an older child, both covered from head to toes with nasty-looking smallpox sores.

"Tell me if you've seen anybody with sores like these," the doctor would plead.

Sometimes, one of the onlookers would show a flicker of recognition on his face, and

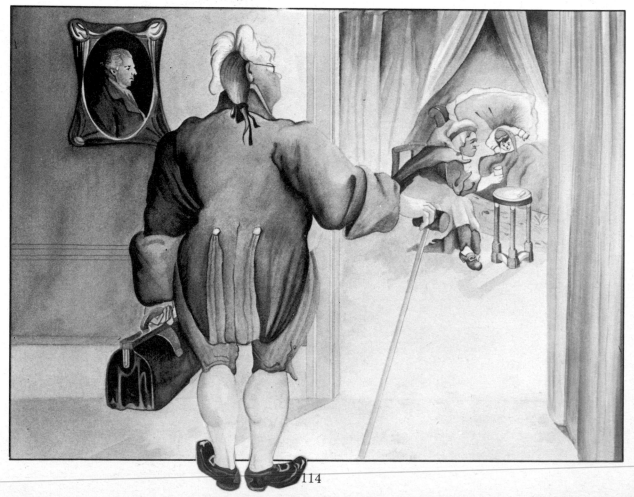

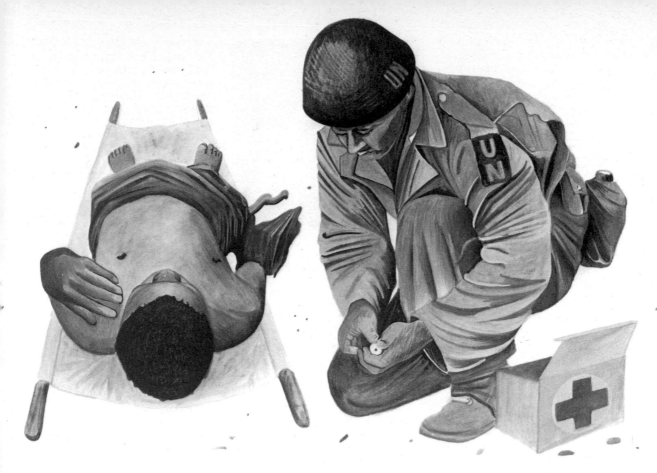

point in the direction of a village in which he had seen somebody with smallpox.

Alarm bells rang in the doctors' minds. Smallpox was in the area. Speedily, they would set up their medical tent and vaccinate everybody in the area. Then they would set off for the village. In most cases they would be too late to save the afflicted child, but they would be in time to save the rest of the villagers, who would be vaccinated to give them immunity to the disease for several years ahead.

Teams such as these have been using up to 250 million doses of vaccine a year to fight the disease which has been a killer from the earliest times — in fact, since history was first recorded.

Certainly, smallpox often gives its victims only the release of death. But if it fails to do this, it can leave them blind or horribly disfigured for life.

Two hundred years ago in Europe, it was common for many children in every community to suffer from smallpox. The potency of the disease so alarmed a British doctor, Edward Jenner, that he devoted

The obliteration of smallpox is the goal of the United Nations who are carrying out a vast vaccination programme.

---

his life to finding a cure for it. He succeeded in 1798 after seeing that milkmaids rarely caught smallpox. However, they did catch a lesser disease called cowpox, and this seemed to make them immune to smallpox.

As an experiment, Jenner took some fluid from a milkmaid's cowpox sore, scratched a boy's arm and put some of the fluid in the scratch. When the child was brought into contact with a smallpox patient, Jenner was jubilant to discover that he did not contract the disease.

This was victory for Jenner — and for mankind as a whole, for it led to the introduction of vaccination and a method of gaining protection from smallpox. But many people chose to spurn it and rejected the opportunity of being vaccinated. It is only in comparatively recent times that the value of preventive medicine has been fully realised and the disease

kept within strict bounds.

Successful though their work has been, the United Nations teams will not be satisfied until their war has been won and the smallpox virus completely eradicated so that the world is free, once and for all, of one of mankind's most dreaded scourges.

With the field troops vaccinating thousands of people a day, it is clear that this is a war with a clear goal — the obliteration of our unseen enemy, the microscopic smallpox virus.

But if a virus escapes the net of the vigilant vaccinators, there is still hope for a person unfortunate enough to catch the disease. With modern drugs, doctors can bring about a cure and thus save a life that might otherwise be lost.

Vaccination is keeping the disease at bay. For people going on holiday to many overseas countries, it is compulsory, and wisely so.

When Edward Jenner made his discovery two hundred years ago, he could hardly have known that he was placing in the hands of doctors a weapon that was to prove to be one of the saviours of the world.

"... we partially turned aside the yet unscrewed lid of the coffin, and looked upon the face of the tenant..."
A SCENE FROM THE FALL OF THE HOUSE OF USHER

MASTER OF THE MACABRE

"AT the request of Usher, I personally aided him in the temporary entombment. The body having been encoffined, we two alone bore it to its rest. The vault in which we placed it was small, damp, and entirely without means for admission of light; lying at great depth, immediately beneath that portion of the building in which was my own sleeping apartment...

"Having deposited our mournful burden upon trestles within this reign of horror, we partially turned aside the yet unscrewed lid of the coffin, and looked upon the face of the tenant.... Our glances, however, rested not long upon the dead –for we could not regard her unawed. The disease which had thus entombed the lady in the maturity of youth, had left ... the mockery of a faint blush upon the bosom and the face, and that suspicious lingering smile which is so terrible in

death. We replaced and screwed down the lid, and, having secured the door of iron, made our way into the scarcely less gloomy apartments of the upper portion of the house...."

If, while reading those words, you felt a slight chill of fear, yet wanted to read on, then the author who wrote them succeeded in his purpose. They are an extract from a short story entitled *The Fall of the House of Usher*, and were written by an American named Edgar Allan

Poe who was born in Boston, Massachussetts, just over 170 years ago, and died aged 43 in 1849.

Poe, although not a prolific writer, has earned a respected place in the world of literature because of his originality, his compelling style of story telling, and above all for his wonderful sense of the mysterious and the macabre.

Even today, when most people are used to horror films, and murder stories, those written by Poe are still as spine-tingling as when they were first published more than a century and a half ago.

In his stories entitled *The Murders in the Rue Morgue*, and *The Mystery of Marie Roget*, Poe created a character he named Auguste Dupin, who was really a forerunner of Sherlock Holmes. These were exciting detective stories with well constructed plots, but Poe added something more–his remarkable power of creating an atmosphere of horror

"... an unusual amount of soot being observed in the fireplace a search was made in the chimney..."
A SCENE FROM MURDER IN THE RUE MORGUE

in his description of blood-curdling scenes.

In *The Murders in the Rue Morgue*, Poe depicts the scene in these words:

"The apartment was in the wildest disorder–the furniture broken and thrown about in all directions. There was only one bedstead; and from this the bed had been removed, and thrown into the middle of the floor. On a chair lay a razor, besmeared with blood. On the hearth were two or three long and thick tresses of grey human hair, also dabbled with blood, and seeming to have been pulled out by the roots. . . .

"Of Madame L'Espanaye no traces were here seen; but an unusual quantity of soot being observed in the fireplace, a search was made in the chimney, and (horrible to relate) the corpse of the daughter, head downward, was dragged therefrom; it having been forced up the narrow aperture for a considerable distance. The body was quite warm.

That story, which formed part of a series of short stories under a heading of *Tales of Mystery and Imagination*, caused quite a sensation when it was first published in 1841. Poe is famed for his mastery of macabre and horror filled narrative but he was well-known also as a poet in his day.

His mother was an English-born actress who had emigrated to the United States. She married another actor, David Poe Jnr. When Edgar was five years old, his mother died and because his father had little money and could not look after him, he was taken into the home of a merchant named John Allan. This is how 'Allan' became added to Poe's other names.

John Allan and his wife cared well, perhaps too well, for the young Edgar who was a rather "sensitive" child. The loss of his parents at such an early age (his father died not long afterwards) must have affected him greatly.

In 1815, the Allans took him to Scotland and to England where he went to the Manor School, Stoke Newington, in London. Five years later he returned to the United States with his foster parents, and Mr. Allan arranged for him to go to the University of Virginia. But unhappily, Edgar developed a liking for gambling and drinking, and he got so much into debt that Mr. Allan refused to support him at the university which parted company with Edgar after only eleven months.

Edgar joined the United States Army under a false name, Edgar A. Perry. Eventually Mr. Allan bought his release and arranged for him to go to the famous military academy at West Point. Finally, because of his continued bad drinking habits, and gambling debts,

"My outstretched hands at length encountered some solid obstruction. It was a wall, seemingly of masonry—very smooth, slimy and cold . . ."
A SCENE FROM THE PIT AND THE PENDULUM

SPRINGETT

Mr. Allan disowned him, and Edgar was expelled from the academy.

By this time, Edgar had already had a book of minor poems published and he now went to New York. There he worked on a number of leading magazines and was, for a brief period, sub-editor of the New York Mirror newspaper which published his poem *The Raven* and some of his short stories. However, his weakness for alcohol gradually caused a deterioration in his health and he developed heart trouble. He died on 7th October, 1849.

Before parting company with this sad, but brilliant genius, let us read an excerpt from another of his short stories. This one is called *The Pit and the Pendulum*, and is a tale of terror about the dreadful tortures that were inflicted on victims of the Spanish Inquisition. Poe tells of how a condemned man finds himself in the pitch blackness of some cold, stone lined dungeon. . . .

". . . I felt nothing, yet dreaded to move a step lest I should be impeded by the walls of a *tomb*. Perspiration burst from every pore, and stood in cold big beads upon my forehead. The agony of suspense grew at length intolerable, and I cautiously moved forward, with my arms extended, and my eyes straining from their sockets in the hope of catching some faint ray of light. . . .

"My outstretched hands at length encountered some solid obstruction. It was a wall, seemingly of stone masonry—very smooth, slimy and cold . . . I had advanced some ten or twelve paces in this manner, when the remnant of the torn hem of my robe became entangled between my legs. I stepped on it, and fell violently on my face. . . .

"I put forward an arm and shudd-ered to find that I had fallen at the very brink of a circular pit whose extent, of course, I had no means of ascertaining at the moment. . . . Groping about the masonry just below the margin, I succeeded in dislodging a small fragment, and let it fall into the abyss. For many seconds I hearkened to its reverberations as it dashed against the sides of the chasm in its descent; at length there was a sullen plunge into water, succeeded by loud echoes. . . . I saw clearly the doom that had been prepared for me. . . . Another step before my fall and the world had seen me no more. . . ."

Horror piles upon horror in *The Pit and the Pendulum* which is probably one of the best examples of the way Poe used the imminent threat of death to cause shivers to run down the spines of his readers.

Definitely not an author to read by candlelight at bedtime!

TRICKSTER WHO CHEATED A CONTINENT

Nobody could have imagined, seeing the frail, prematurely-aged woman in her cell in a convent in Rome that she had once been a dazzling beauty, the envy of all the high-born ladies of Europe.

But there had been a price to be paid for her fame and for the fortune that had been won and lost. The strain that accompanied the earning of them, had left its price etched deeply in her face in the furrows on her brow and the hollows in her cheeks.

From eyes sunk deeply in their sockets, she gazed dully at a robed priest, who was setting out his parchment and quill pen on a desk in the corner of the cell by the light of a flickering candle.

"Madame," murmured the priest. "You have told us about your life with the man who calls himself the Count of Cagliostro. It is incredible . . . amazing."

"I swear that I have spoken nothing but the truth," whispered the woman.

"Then, I think you should make a full confession, which I will write down and present to the fathers who are conducting the inquisition. They will decide if the Count is to be condemned as a heretic and what his fate shall be—death or life imprisonment."

Perhaps there was a malicious smile on the woman's parched lips as she nodded and began her startling story of her life with the Count of Cagliostro, the most barefaced and successful confidence trickster Europe had ever known.

For years, the Count and his beautiful wife, whom he called the Countess Serafina, had been fêted as the wonder couple of Europe. They had moved in high society. Kings, princes, lords, nobles and cardinals all accepted them as miracle workers and paid them fortunes for their cures and elixirs that were supposed to ensure eternal youth.

To convince them, the Countess Serafina had

The woman seated before the priest told an amazing story of how she had played her part in the life of one of the world's most daring tricksters.

pretended to be 60 when, in fact, she was 30, hoping to persuade her gullible and over-rich clients that eternal youth was within the reach of all who could afford to pay for the Count's elixir. Such things did not seem impossible to these 18th century people, who had heard of the Count's ability to turn lead into gold, change coarse cotton into beautifully smooth silk and double the size of a diamond. He could even enable invalids to recover from illnesses that the best doctors had pronounced as incurable.

Who was this miracle worker? In his time, Cagliostro had used many names, but the one with which he had been born in Palermo in Sicily in 1743 was Giuseppe Balsamo. He received scant shooling at the hands of some local monks, who taught him a little about chemistry.

But Cagliostro had his eye on bigger things. With money stolen from the church poor box and his uncle's savings—also stolen—Cagliostro set out to make his fortune. In 1768, he was in Rome selling beauty creams and potions which he mixed himself. He also proved expert at forging the paintings of such masters as Rembrandt. He forged bonds, bank notes and even wills which were so expertly executed that when some were tested by a court of law, the court was completely taken in and declared that they were genuine.

Then began Cagliostro's notorious partnership with the lady in the cell. Her real name was Lorenza Feliciani, and she was born in the slums of Rome. When Cagliostro met and married her she was 15, and together they embarked upon a life of deception and trickery. For ten years they wandered around Europe and North Africa preying upon the rich and gullible.

LIFE OF LUXURY

By 1777, when they came to London, they had amassed £3,000 and were able to live a life of luxury with what was then a fortune. It was then that the pair took on their titles of Count Alessandro di Cagliostro and his beautiful wife, Countess Serafina. To add a touch of Eastern mysticism, Cagliostro said that he had stolen his wife from an Oriental harem.

To gain a foothold in London society, Cagliostro joined a London lodge of the Freemasonry movement, which was then spreading all over Europe with the greatest and grandest men as members. Persuading the London members to elect him Grand Master, Cagliostro then began travelling in great style all over Europe.

Elegant coaches provided Cagliostro with his setting of apparent wealth, as did his own rich apparel and his bevy of servants in spectacular livery. The Countess, herself, wore the most elegant clothes and was adorned with the finest gems.

All this was the window dressing for Cagliostro's business of deceiving the gullible. Everywhere he went, he was greeted as the visiting Grand Master of a respected London lodge. If anybody asked where his money came from, he told them the tale about being able to turn lead into gold and double diamonds in size. His hearers, too, could learn how to perform these miracles if they were willing to pay the high price demanded for the secret processes. By the time they had tried them and discovered that they were worthless, Cagliostro had passed on to another town and a further set of credulous nobles.

Cagliostro became an expert at forging works of art.

Cagliostro invented a kind of Freemasonry with himself at the head. He was called the Grand Cophta, and all the fees and dues went into his own pocket. At the head of the female branch was his wife, whom he now called the Queen of Sheba. In Paris, where they conducted this deception, rich and titled ladies scrambled to join, lured on by Cagliostro's promise to share his secrets with them. He kept his promise, but at a high price, for most of the cures involved strange elixirs which only Cagliostro could supply. And he never sold anything cheaply.

What these secret potions contained is not known, for very few formulas have survived, though he is thought to have made use of herbal medicines. For the rich, however, he wrapped his pills in gold leaf, which made the ingredients appear rare and expensive to justify his high price.

Cagliostro's downfall began with his meeting with Louis de Rohan, the Prince Cardinal of Strasbourg. Then came some deception over a diamond necklace, which is worth a story in itself. The upshot was that Rohan, Cagliostro and the "countess" were imprisoned in France, where their intrigue had taken place.

After a trial, Cagliostro and his wife were released. But their glory had now faded. Nobody wanted to know them. Poverty-stricken, near to starvation, they went to Rome, where their past caught up with them with a vengeance.

Cagliostro was a Roman Catholic and, as such, was forbidden to become a Freemason. Because of this, he was arrested and denounced as a heretic.

And it was while he was in prison that Cagliostro's wife, who was imprisoned in the convent, began to make a full confession of their lives of deceit and theft.

THE SENTENCE

When she had finished, the priest who had been writing it all down, picked up his parchments and left the cell, his face full of infinite sadness for those who had been deceived by the heartless couple.

But the questions and the probings were not over yet. For 15 months the inquisition continued. Then, at last, on 7th April, 1791, the inquisition announced its findings. Cagliostro would be sentenced to death as a heretic. Due to the pope's mercy, this sentence was being reduced to one of life imprisonment.

And so the confidence trickster who had had all of Europe at his feet was put into a grim, grey cell in the impregnable fortress of San Leo where the guards never ceased their vigilance to keep him firmly behind the bars.

On 26th August, 1795, the prison bell began tolling its mournful notes to tell all within earshot that a death had occurred within its walls. The end had come at last to Cagliostro, who was only 52 years old.

In those comparatively few years, he had packed enough adventure and excitement to fill a score of books. For although the world has never been short of tricksters, there has never been any to rival Cagliostro for his flair, audacity and sheer success as the confidence trickster who fooled them all from kings and cardinals down to the rich businessmen who were willing to pay for the dreams he peddled with his potions and elixirs. Truly, he was the champion trickster of all times.

Dressed in fine clothes and riding in splendid coaches, the Count and his wife appeared to have all the trappings of wealth.

BELLMAN TO THE RESCUE

THE fog swept in from the sea, grey, cold and wet, it blotted out the landscape. It crept over Bodmin Moor.

Andrew and Jane sat shoulder to shoulder beneath the overhang of a big boulder on Rough Tor. Nine year-old Jane was trying hard not to cry, but Andrew could feel her muffled sobs against his shoulder. He was three years older than Jane. Both children were wet and cold and hungry, and they were lost in the vastness of the moor. They gazed into the fog. Ten yards away the tumbled boulders of the tor were invisible.

"I'm so cold," said Jane.

"Somebody will find us," said Andrew. "We must stay here. The moor isn't safe. There are bogs and things."

"Its getting darker," whispered Jane. Both children knew that night was coming.

With their father, Mr. Tregunna, they had been out hunting. Hounds had found a fox in a patch of gorse. Andrew and Jane had soon been left behind by the rest of the field on their bigger horses. They had been enjoying themselves scampering along on their long-tailed moorland ponies. Both of them knew the country well. They knew their way home. Jane's pony had put a foot into a disused rabbit hole, and she had fallen heavily, badly winded. Her pony galloped on and Andrew had gone to his sister's aid. As he bent down to lift her he let go of his mount's reins, and the pony had galloped after his stable companion. It was then that the children noticed the bank of fog advancing from the north. Their ponies disappeared over the skyline. When Jane could walk, the children set out in the direction of the main road, but the fog came down. They were lost. Rough Tor towered above them, and they made for it to get above the bogs and moorland streams.

"If only we had the ponies," said Andrew, "they would take us home."

He and Jane had already eaten the sandwiches which they had brought with them.

"It'll be all right Janey," said Andrew. "Somebody will find us," but he was frightened.

"Listen," gulped his sister.

Both children leaned forward. A bird, somewhere below them in the fog, gave a double, fluting cry.

"Curlew," said Andrew.

"Not that," Jane said. "Listen."

From far away came the deep yodelling music of a hunting fox hound.

"Its Bellman," said Jane excitedly.

Both children knew all the hounds in the pack, but Bellman was their special friend. They had looked after him when he was a young puppy, and had won first prize with him for the best kept hound at the annual puppy show. They had been sad when he had to be returned to the hunt kennels. They loved him dearly.

"Bellman, Bellman," yelled the children, but their voices were swallowed by the fog.

He was the most handsome hound in the pack, but his chief glory was the music of his voice. He was well named Bellman. It is sad to relate however, that as a hunter of foxes, Bellman was useless. The Master had said, for a long time that the pack must be rid of him, for poor Bellman was a babbler. That is, he would give tongué to the scent of a rabbit, a deer, or even a pheasant. The Master was sure that Bellman would speak to the line of a field mouse. Bellman took little interest in foxes.

We shall never know what Bellman thought he was hunting in thick fog, at four o'clock of a winter evening.

His voice came more clearly to the shivering children, huddled against the boulder.

"Yooi," Andrew called as he got to his feet "Bellman, Bellman, Here boy."

Suddenly the big hound was there. He fell upon the children liking them ecstatically, whining with joy at finding the friends of his youth. His arrival gave the children courage. Now they saw a chance of getting safely home. Andrew took off his long hunting stock, and tied it round Bellman's neck. The hound was hungry and eager to go home. Any home would do, so long as it would provide food. The children stumbled down the hillside, Andrew holding Bellman with one hand, and clutching Jane with the other. Often they fell, but Andrew held firmly to the end of the stock round Bellman's neck.

There was the sound of water trickling, as the hound lead them safely over a stone bridge. Now they were on a rough road, between high banks which showed more darkly than the foggy night. A light shone dimly, a weak yellow haze in the blackness. Bellman snuffled his way to the front door of the house from which the light came. Soon the children and the hound were in a car, driving slowly homewards.

Andrew and Jane, warm and sleepy after hot baths, were eating their supper in front of a roaring fire. Bellman lay asleep on the hearth, sometimes whimpering as he hunted some small creature in his dreams. Certainly it would not have been a fox.

The children listened to their father who was speaking on the telephone to the Master of Fox Hounds. They could hear the hearty shouts which came from the other end.

"No," roared the Master in a tinny rattling voice. "I don't want him back. Give him to the children."

"Oh!" gasped Jane, and tears of joy rolled down her cheeks. She was very tired.

Now, Bellman spends the cold winter afternoons in front of the fire, or hunts starlings in the shrubbery. No more stupid fox hunting. No more angry whippers-in with cracking whip thongs, and their everlasting "Bellman—Gerraway on to it."

With Andrew's long hunting stock tied to his neck, Bellman set off through the fog.

THE SPANIARDS'

THE watchers on the shore saw fortified castles that moved on the ocean. Out of these castles came black-bearded men with white faces who had terrible weapons that spat flame and belched smoke and killed enemies a long way off, while – wonders of wonders – many of these alarming strangers were mounted on beasts that looked like deer.

These "stags" snorted and bellowed and sweated. Foam came from their mouths and they made a loud noise on the ground when they ran, leaving marks and scars where they had passed over it. . . .

Such was the impact on Mexican Indians when the Spaniard Cortés landed his small army on the coast in 1519, seeking gold and bound for the fabulous city of Mexico. There were no horses in the Americas and not for the first or last time in history were horses to prove highly effective "secret weapons."

For the story of the horse is a series of turning points. No one knows when, where or how it was first domesticated, but we do know where it happened, records proving that it was tamed on the steppes of southern Russia to the north of the Black Sea and the Caspian Sea some 5,000 or more years ago. Chariots – a giant step forward – are mentioned around 1,800 B.C., and within a thousand years, the Aryans, who had first domesticated the horse, had descended with invincible war chariots into Mesopotamia, a turning point indeed, for it was the equivalent of using repeating rifles on spear-throwing natives. By 1,500 B.C. the horse chariot was in action throughout the ancient world. By now, too, horses were widely used for riding, the sequence being probably first using horses as food, then driving them, and finally – a magical moment – riding them.

War and hunting were the chief uses of horses in the early days, but a veil of mystery hangs over much of their story until 890 B.C. when records prove that cavalry was used by the Assyrians to wipe out the army of the King of Nairi. Gone were the days when horses were small, quiet ponies, for now they were being bred for war and work, and looked it. The ancient Greeks improved things by going in for horse racing in a big way.

The Romans made little use of cavalry, preferring to depend on their matchless legions of infantry, and the next major turning point came when the most terrifying horsemen in history swept out of the wastes of Mongolia.

These were the dreaded Huns, who virtually lived on horseback and are credited with the invention of the stirrup around A.D. 500, 2,000 years after the bit had been evolved in the Middle East. With the stirrup, riding became faster and horsemen could travel further without strain, while even the fattest men could mount their horses more easily.

Now our story returns to where

Among the many strange and terrifying things which Cortés and his men brought to Mexico was the horse, an animal unknown to the Aztecs.

SECRET WEAPON

it began, in the New World in the 16th century where turning points, often well-documented, came thick and fast, as they were bound to in vast continents which had never been trodden by horses' hooves.

If the impact of Cortés's horses on the Mexican Indians was tremendous, as he overthrew the Aztec empire based on Mexico City, it was even more staggering on the Incas of Peru. In 1532, a Spanish adventurer named Francisco Pizarro, a distant kinsman of Cortés, but a far less admirable man, set out with 177 men and 37 horses to conquer the vast Inca Empire. The Incas were a small ruling class who governed what is now Peru, Ecuador, Bolivia and part of Chile, and were all powerful rulers, less crue than the Aztecs of Mexico whom Cortés overthrew, but equally advanced. Though they had not invented the wheel, they built fine roads, impressive buildings and farmed scientifically, while lording it over 15 million people, all of whom knew their place in the order of things. At the "top of the heap" of this benevolent dictatorship was the Sun God, the Emperor Atahualpa.

These gifted people were overthrown by daring, treachery, luck and two secret weapons, gunpowder and the horse. The last weapon made a big impression from the very outset. In an early skirmish soon after they had anchored, a horde of warriors were thrown into total confusion when a Spaniard became separated from his horse. The natives had though that man and beast were one, and this happened time and time again. The Inca rulers were harder to impress, but were astounded by the horses. Pizarro and his men marched unharmed through the country, however, and were received with friendship, finally meeting Atahualpa. Hernando de Soto, Pizarro's second-in command, decided to impress the Sun God as he sat on a throne to greet the strangers, and began to show off by indulging in a tremendous display of horsemanship, which ended by a headlong gallop straight at Athualpa. Inches from him, de Soto drew up, the Sun God having not moved a muscle, but some of his courtiers were terrified and were later executed for cowardice.

Later, Pizarro treacherously murdered Atahualpa after capturing him and extracting a gigantic ransom in gold for him, and with their god dead, the Incas lost their will to resist and let a handful of men conquer millions.

For our final turning point in the story of the horse, we move northwards, where harsh Spanish soldiers set out to explore the even harsher landscape of what is now the American Southwest. With them, and the troops and settlers who followed, went the cattle who were to be the ancestors of the longhorns the Texas cowboys knew, and horses.

In all North America there were no horses, and the million or so Red Indians were either primitive farmers, or wanderers. Without the horse the lives of nomads were hard indeed, especially on the great plains and prairies. Possessions were carried or dragged by dogs on travois far smaller than were later dragged by horses. Only Indians living by water could move freely and fast.

In the West the buffalo was all important, providing them with food, shelter and clothing, but hunting the buffalo on foot was a slow, often dangerous business, which meant that food was hard to come by.

As the number of horses grew and spread northwards, tribe after tribe began to tame them.

This situation changed, because some of the Spanish horses ran wild and multiplied. So it came about that from the mid-16th century onwards, the horse spread northwards, and tribe after tribe discovered the wonderful creature and tamed it. By 1750, horses had spread all over the West, some coming in from French Canada in the Northeast, but there were grim moments for those tribes which had not yet become mounted. After centuries of war on foot, a neighbouring tribe which already had the horse, was likely to sweep down and overwhelm the opposition.

More peacefully, the buffalo hunt became a marvellous event, not simply because food was easier to come by, but because it was now so exciting, almost as exciting as war.

So the life of the American Indian was transformed. We think of him as a warrior on a horse, proud and erect, yet only for a century and a half or so was this picture the true one. The 'dog days' when the tribes were on foot are forgotten. The Indians became great guerilla fighters, some of the finest light cavalry in the world.

Was there yet another turning point in horse history? The invention of the automobile must surely rank as the final one, when horses ceased to be mankind's principal beast of burden; but, happily man and horse are as strongly linked as ever. There will be no more turning points, just a strong relationship which will survive as long as mankind.